The Universal Healing Art of JING-QI-SHEN

A Complete Guide to Hands-On Healing

By Rinchen Chodak

Jing-Qi-Shen Foundation Press
Lake Elsinore, CA

Jing-Qi-Shen Foundation Press
Lake Elsinore, California

www.jing-qi-shen.org
Email: info@jing-qi-shen.org

ISBN 978-0-6151-3695-0

Note to the reader: This book is not intended as a substitute for the medical recommendations of physicians or other health-care providers. Rather, it is intended to offer information to help the reader cooperate with physicians and health professionals in a mutual quest for optimum well-being.

Cover Art Description: Human Hand print with the Taoist symbol, a single circular black ink brush stroke indicating wholeness, completeness, and infinity. The Chinese character in the upper left corner means "Health".

This book is dedicated with love to my teacher Chetsang Xian Rinposhe, and to all Jing-Qi-Shen students, past, present and future. May your ministry of health and wholeness continue to bloom and to flourish. Namaste and many blessings to you all.

Invocation of the Medicine Buddha

Om namo bhagawate beshajye guru,
Vaidurya prabha rajaya Tathagataya
Arhte sammyaksam Buddhaya Tadyatha
Om Bheshajye Beshajye maha Beshajye
Beshajye rajaya samungate svaha

May all beings be auspicious! I make my prostration to you who destroyed the enemy of negative life cycle changes, who has thus gone to the state of enlightenment like other Buddhas, who perfectly accomplished the quality of the Buddha, the Supreme Physician who is fully liberated and awakened, the Enlightened One, Medicine Buddha. Bedurya, King of the Physicians.

Table of Contents

FORWARD

I met Dar Umemoto in the Spring of 2003. The truth is that I had been anticipating our meeting for almost 70 years. When I entered the Monastery as a young novice, my Master would have me offer up incense and pujas (prayers) daily for those who were predestined to join me in this lifetime. So, here I was, 70 years later, standing in a small room, as Dar was being ushered in to meet me.

At the time of our first meeting, Dar had just begun studying the Healing Arts at a small Asian healing clinic located in Southern California. I was told that she was an exceptional student, was naturally intuitive, and that she had a naturally innate understanding of how to manipulate universal energy. I was quite intrigued when I also learned that she was a westerner. I sat waiting patiently for my friend and colleague Dr. Ming to bring her to the small reception room of the temple. The door opened, and in walked Dr. Ming with Dar following closely behind tripping over her robes as she walked. She looked at me with widened eyes and burst out into laughter as she bowed to me. I liked her instantly, appreciating her laughing heart, and then had a knowing that our meeting was indeed predestined.

I began to privately tutor her in the Healing Arts and in the basic precepts of Buddhism as much as my time permitted, and later in a peaceful ceremony, gave her a spiritual name. Rinchen Chodak, The Jewel Who Shows The Way.

Rinchen began to teach a small group of other students the energy healing art I learned from my teacher which was simply called "Qi Hand, Qi Breath". Rinchen continued to study the healing art diligently, along with other healing arts in general, updating and refining what she learned like one who polishes a rough stone. I am pleased with Rinchen's new name for the art as I believe it aptly describes its essence. Jing-Qi-Shen is a new name for an old healing art which has been passed down through the generations.

I have given Rinchen the task of relieving suffering by presenting an avenue towards health and wholeness that the entire world can walk. This is an honorable task, and one that I am certain Rinchen Chodak, and all of the students who complete this instruction course, will pursue with compassion.

Namaste,

Chetsang Xian, DOM
Singapore, September 7, 2006

AUTHOR'S INTRODUCTION

The year I was born, President Lyndon B. Johnson signed the Civil Rights Act of 1964. Nelson Mandela was sentenced to life imprisonment in South Africa as a result of his opposition to apartheid. Jack Ruby was convicted of the murder of Lee Harvey Oswald, China detonated its first atomic bomb, and the Beatles made their first appearance on the Ed Sullivan show.

I grew up in a traditional American home, was raised in a traditional city suburb, and attended a traditional public school. I went to college, received a degree in Paralegal Sciences, and then went on to attend and graduate from law school. I was a typical American citizen, living a typical American life, until I had an untypical spiritual awakening.

I emerged from my spiritual awakening feeling like I was born anew in thought and form. At that time my teacher Chetsang Xian Rinposhe bestowed upon me a new name. From that day forward I was known as Rinchen Chodak, which means The Jewel Who Shows The Way.

Although I have received much of my experience in the healing arts from a group of Tibetan Monks operating a small Asian healing center, and although I embrace and practice many of the Buddha's teachings, I am not Buddhist. I have a deep understanding of the Christian Holy Bible, but I do not consider myself religious. I suppose I can say that I am a contemporary spiritual teacher who is not aligned to any particular religion or tradition.

Aside from being Buddhist Monks, my healing teachers were Doctor's of Oriental Medicine, Allopathic Physicians, Acupuncturists, Chinese Herbalists, and Naturopathic Medical Doctors. This manual is the result of the time and effort that all of my beloved teachers invested in me as their student.

What is Jing-Qi-Shen? Jing-Qi-Shen is named after the San Bao, or Three Treasures, common in Traditional Chinese Medicine. The English translation would be Essence-Energy-Spirit. Known and taught to my teacher as simply "Qi Hands, Qi Breath", Jing-Qi-Shen combines elements of the Meridian System as found in Traditional Chinese Medicine, Energy Healing, and Medical Intuition. Jing-Qi-Shen affects the auric, etheric, and physical layers of the body through intuitive projection of light, sound, chakra rebalancing, auric cleansing, direct and indirect touch, meridian work, and intuitive scanning of the body. It is also a deeply compassionate and peaceful healing art, teaching the practitioner the importance of moving aside personal ego in order to be a pure, loving conduit of Universal Healing Energy.

I am honored and deeply touched that I have been given the task of introducing The Universal Healing Art of Jing-Qi-Shen to the western world and abroad. As I embark on my wonderful journey of teaching this beloved art to the masses, I welcome you join me as a kindred spirit, and as a Minister of Healing. Our Mission – to bring health and wholeness to the world.

PART ONE

Introduction to Healing Theory

I believe that a brief introduction into the theory of healing; it's essence, it's definition, and it's composition, is an important part of not only administering healing to others, but also in receiving a healing response with in your self. The theories presented in this section are applicable regardless of the energy healing modality being used.

The first section of the text will give you a brief introduction to the concepts of healing as taught in Traditional Chinese Medicine (TCM). This includes the definition of illness or disease from a TCM practitioner's standpoint, as well as TCM's concept of healing energy through the three treasures: Jing, Qi, and Shen.

We will then unravel the science of healing energy as explained through basic scientific principles in order to understand how energy healing works.

A thorough understanding of the information as presented in the following chapters will provide you with a strong foundation on which to build your healing repertoire.

CHAPTER ONE

TRADITIONAL CHINESE MEDICINE & JING-QI-SHEN

Traditional Chinese Medicine (TCM) treats the human body as a fundamental system of integrated networks, each having its own unique physiological function. This united system uses energy pathways to link the organs and the other systems of the body together as a unified whole, thus allowing communication and interaction between all of the body organs possible. The energy that flows along these energy pathways is called qi (pronounced "chee").

These qi pathways make up what are called energy meridians. Meridians are classified into two groups: the "Zheng Jing", or primary meridians, and the "Ji Jing", or secondary meridians. The primary meridians flow directly to the major internal organs, while the secondary do not.

There are twelve primary meridians and eight secondary, from which are derived even smaller pathways such as meridian extensions, collaterals, and sub-collaterals.

Meridians can be accessed externally through acupuncture and acupressure points, which are points located on the skin that connect to the channels or vessels. Stimulation of these points connect with the energy pathways which then connects directly or indirectly to the organs, which then affects the flow of qi from and through the organs.

When the body is injured or an illness occurs, the symptoms that result are dependant upon the condition of qi in the body. Illness or injury manifests as either deficient qi or stagnant qi. Deficient qi refers to a weakness in the function of the body or organ system. Stagnant qi refers to a restricted flow of qi in the body.

When the energies in the meridian system are abundant and flowing harmoniously, physiological functions operate efficiently, eliminating causes of illness. If a person becomes sick, the illness can remedied by restoring the flow of vital qi in the body. So where then does illness originate?

TCM has classified energy as used in medicine in many ways. The most common explanation can be found in the Three Treasures (San Bao) – jing (essence-of-life), qi (energy), and shen (spirit). It is believed that the Three Treasures, jing, qi, and shen, are the fundamental building blocks for all facets of life. An imbalance in any of the three will influence the others and can result in disease or illness within the body.

Although jing, qi, and shen can be richly explained in metaphysical terms, let's take a look at each of the Three Treasures from the standpoint of TCM.

Jing.

Defined in TCM as essence-of-life, jing is considered to be the fundamental material that comprises the physical body. In modern western terminology, it is the subatomic particles that make up all of our bodily parts. TCM classifies jing into two separate categories; innate jing, and acquired jing.

Innate-jing is the essence inherited from our parents on a genetic level. Acquired-jing is essence obtained through food and water. Acquired-jing is assimilated in the digestive system and converted, storing any excess in the kidneys along with innate-jing. Both acquired and innate jing mutually support one another. Acquired-jing is the essential substance needed for the proper functioning of all bodily activities and the metabolism. A living organism cannot survive without food and water. Jing is continually used and being restored by food and water, with any surplus stored in the kidneys.

When jing supply is abundant your vitality is strong providing a safeguard to prevent illness. When jing is deficient, your vitality is weak and your immune system will be compromised.

Qi.

Qi is the essential substance that permeates and creates the cosmos. It includes the energy derived from air, food, water, as well as the hereditary energy we receive from our parents.

The Chinese believe that the human body is a complete miniature of the cosmos and stress the relationship between human beings and elemental forces, both local (or environmental), and cosmic. Ancient Chinese philosophers viewed human qi as the result of the interaction between the qi of heaven (yang), and the qi of earth (yin). This relationship, cosmically and locally, teaches us that we are constantly influenced by the natural rhythms and cycles in our environment (lunar and solar); and that we can be susceptible to conditions created by the surrounding climate, such as wind, cold, damp, heat, summer heat, and dryness.

In addition to this, TCM teaches:

1. Qi manifests itself physically, mentally, and spiritually.
2. Qi changes form according to its locality and function.
3. There are many varieties of qi in living beings; however there is only one qi source manifesting itself into these many forms.
4. Qi is in a constant state of flux causing its material and in material shape to vary. When qi condenses down, it solidifies to form a physical shape. An example of this is tumors or cysts resulting from an imbalance of qi circulating throughout the body.

THE FIVE FUNCTIONS OF QI IN THE BODY

Qi Function	What it does
Movement	Is in constant motion entering and leaving the body through willed, physical, involuntary, and mental actions: Eating, talking, and laughing (willed actions); Exercising, walking, and cleaning the house, (physical actions); Blood flow, breathing, heartbeat (involuntary actions); Artistic creation, thinking, day dreaming (mental actions).
Protection	Balances, stabilizes, and enhances immune system from internal and external harmful influences such as excessive wind, cold, fire, heat, dampness, and dryness.
Warmth	Balances and maintains normal heat in the body and its organs.
Transformation	Transforms ingested food into other states such as sweat, blood, tears.
Stability & Retention	Maintains physical structure of the body and its internal organs, and assures that all bodily systems maintain their assigned biological structure.

Qi flows through the meridian system of the body, through the blood and makes up the cells in the body. It is a refined substance produced by the internal organs to nourish the mind, body, and soul. The form Qi takes varies according to its location and function. TCM teaches that there are five basic functions of Qi within the physical body. In its most basic components, qi protects the body, warms the body, is the source of all movement, accompanies all movement, is the source of harmonious transformation, ensures stability, and finally, governs retention.

There are many functions and forms of qi categorized in TCM, however for this text we will define qi as a refined substance produced in the internal organs to nourish the body, mind and spirit, and as the original creative substance before All That Is.

Shen.

Shen is loosely translated as "Spirit". It is the Guiding Spirit that directs qi. Shen is ultimately the most important of the Three Treasures since it reflects our connection to our higher nature above the classification of a simple human being. The Chinese masters state that Shen is the deep, pure love for all totality that resides our hearts. Shen is the essence-of-essence, the perfect and refined substance of the Universe. It expresses itself through selfless love, kindness, compassion, forgiveness and generosity. It is that higher knowledge of the All-That-Is; interconnected and manifest as One.

When there is a deficiency is Shen it is easily noticed in the eyes which are often said to be the "mirror to the soul". Bright, expressive eyes reveal the deep vitality of Spirit, while dull, lackluster eyes the opposite.

Deficient Shen also manifests through repressed or hyper emotional states such as anger, anxiety, grief, or sadness. It is not that these emotions in themselves are "bad" as they do have a balanced place in certain circumstances of everyday living. However, numerous medical studies have proven that dominating, long-term emotions can indeed be the major source of ill health.

Summary of Chapter:

- TCM looks at the human body as an integrated system comprised of energy pathways or meridians. Each meridian has it's own unique function within the body,
- The energy that flows along these energy pathways is call qi.
- Meridians can be accesses directly through acupuncture and acupressure points located on the skin, or indirectly through "energy medicine" modalities.
- TCM classifies energy used in Chinese Medicine as San Bao, or the Three Treasures: Jing (Essence-of-Life), Qi (Energy), and Shen (Spirit).
- Jing, Qi, and Shen are the fundamental building blocks for all facets of life. An imbalance in any of the three can result in illness or disease.

CHAPTER TWO

THE SCIENCE OF ENERGY HEALING

The Energy Healing Arts are no longer a mystery. Various documented studies have been able to explain the Energy Healing arts through basic scientific principles. These studies have proved the existence of the aura, an energy field that surrounds all living things. They have confirmed that human intention itself could be utilized as a potent healing force, that the Energy Healing Arts could affect and influence cancer cells, could heal laboratory animals, could influence the growth rate of bacteria, and even realign the physical substructure of the human body.

These studies were also able to determine one or more shared characteristics of the healers who participated in the study. These similarities were existent regardless of the healing modality being used.

Among these common qualities was the belief or intention of the person facilitating the healing that they could affect a change in the patients body, the use of relaxation, visualization and affirmation techniques (most importantly of the patient in perfect health), calling upon a higher Spiritual Power for assistance, and the giving of thanksgiving to this Spiritual Source for assistance.

What then are the principles which explain how a healing response inside the patient occurs? One of the most fascinating aspects of my own training in the Energetic Healing Arts was learning how energy healing actually worked.

The human body can be described as an oscillating system. An oscillator is any object that moves in a regular, periodic manner. It is anything that vibrates, or performs a repetitive periodic movement. If we placed two tuned guitars near one another and strummed one of the strings, the sting on the neighboring guitar tuned in the same key would begin to vibrate. When the guitar string is struck it will produce a transfer of energy in the form of sound waves which the similarly tuned guitar string absorbs, causing it to vibrate to its own natural frequency. A system made of two tuned oscillators is called a resonant system.

We can explain a resonant system in many ways but the most memorable example I was given was that of several grandfather clocks lined up along a single wall. At first the free swinging pendulum would move out of sync with one another. But, as a result of the energy moving through the wall from clock to clock, within a short period of time the pendulums would match the rhythm of one another, swinging in unison.

The process of one oscillator that "matches" the vibration of a similar oscillating system is called rhythm entrainment. The fastest oscillator, the one that is vibrating at the highest rate, will force the slower oscillators to occur in phase with one another, lifting its vibrational frequency, or "entraining" them to operate at the higher rate.

Tuning forks are also a great demonstration of rhythm and entrainment. A tuning fork struck in one key vibrates sound waves. A nearby tuning fork in the same key will match the vibration and entrain to it causing sound to emit.

A resonant system is not limited to non-living systems. Documented laboratory studies have shown that when a dissected (still beating) frog heart is placed in the proximity of another freshly dissected frog heart that they will begin to beat in unison within a short period of time. I find this quite fascinating.

I often marvel when I drive along the Southern California freeways at rush hour. I can always notice the drivers entraining to the lower vibration of other drivers. We can also notice this when standing in line at the grocery store. The feeling of impatience entrains into others operating at the same frequency or lower. Such unconscious living saddens me. It seems prudent that we should always attempt to maintain the highest frequency possible in activities of everyday living.

In many healing modalities, Jing-Qi-Shen included, the healing facilitator is taught to raise his or her vibration through rhythmic breathing, toning, mantra, visualization, and meditative techniques. The healing facilitator is taught to keep raising his or her energy vibration creating a strong resonance in the receiver causing rhythm entrainment, or the matching of the facilitator's energy vibration. Healing then occurs as the client's body raises up and matches it's frequency to that of the facilitator.

In his book *Stalking the Wild Pendulum*, Itzhak Bentov states, "We may look at a disease as such out-of-tune behavior of one or another of our organs in the body. When a strong harmonizing rhythm is applied to it, the interfering pattern of waves, which is the organ, may start beating in tune again. This may be the principle of psychic healing."

Summary of Chapter:

- The human body is an oscillating system.
- A system made of two tuned oscillators is called a resonant system.
- A resonant system is not limited to non-living systems.
- The Energy Healing Arts can be explained by the principles of sound or vibration, resonance, and rhythm entrainment.
- Studies have shown that energy healers have one or more of the following in common: the belief or intention that the patient could be healed, calling upon or connecting to a higher Spiritual Power for assistance, visualization and affirmation of the patient in perfect health, and thanksgiving to a higher Spiritual Power for assistance.

PART TWO

The Basic Concepts of Jing-Qi-Shen

The following chapters are the meat and potatoes of this text. It is suggested that the student read each chapter as many times as needed, and to not overlook the exercises provided. Through out this course we will continue to emphasis the importance of consistent practice. Jing-Qi-Shen is a skill. As with all learned skills, practice makes perfect.

CHAPTER THREE

FREQUENTLY ASKED QUESTIONS ABOUT JING-QI-SHEN

The following questions are the most commonly asked questions by students new to Jing-Qi-Shen (JQS). I believe that these questions provide a great mental springboard for the student before embarking on their journey through Part Two.

What illnesses or diseases can benefit from a JQS healing session?

To answer this question it is first necessary to remember that JQS classifies all disease or illness as deficient or excessive energy which has condensed, or solidified in a particular area of the body.

Through out my years of study, and through facilitating hundreds of healings, I have seen many remarkable and sometimes miraculous shifts in a client's bio-energetic body during and after a healing session. Among the miraculous, I have seen and felt bones realign themselves under my fingertips, and have even felt a solid tumor mass shrink before my eyes.

JQS is safe to use on any condition presented to you. Common complaints of clients who have come to me for healing facilitations are muscle pains and injuries, broken bones, colds, flu, edema, TMJ, cysts, migraine headaches, depression, female issues, and gastritis and other digestive issues. A great number of clients come to me for general wellness treatments in order to keep their bio-energetic body clean and balanced.

Is JQS a new healing art, or a facsimile of other energy healing arts?

The energy healing arts have been known to be in existence in the ancient cultures of China, India, and Tibet. The energy healing arts are Universal, each operating in such a way as to elevate the vibration of the client b sensing and clearing stagnant energy in the etheric and physical bodies; as well as using various techniques to generate and send healing energy to their clients. Due to the close proximity of China, India, and Tibet, it is not surprising that the healing arts found in those cultures today share similarities.

Jing-Qi-Shen is a new name for an old healing art taught to my teacher. When I first encountered this healing art my teacher Xian Rinposhe simply called it "Qi Hand, Qi Breath".

Is JQS more effective than other healing arts?

All energy healing arts are effective. One particular style of energy healing art is not necessarily better than another. To believe so is an attempt for the ego mind to set itself above and apart from others. All energy healing arts have emerged from the Essence-of-Essence; The Divine Pool of Universal Consciousness. The only difference in any healing art is the skill of each individual practitioner.

Does a JQS Practitioner need to receive energy attunements before they are able to give a healing session?

No. JQS does not require energy attunements nor are they necessary for someone to effectively learn to draw and send healing Qi.

Can anyone learn JQS?

Yes, anyone can learn JQS. Self-study students and workshop participants come from all walks of life including: home executives, school teachers, members of the clergy, chiropractors, holistic health practitioners, massage professionals, physical therapists, physicians, and nurses.

How long does it take to learn JQS?

JQS workshop intensives are two days in length, and the self-study course may take up to three months to complete. However, as with any skill, continual practice is vital for the effectiveness of a JQS practitioner.

The Jing-Qi-Shen Foundation requires each student and workshop participant a minimum of 80 hours of healing facilitations before considering a student proficient in the basic essentials of JQS. We suggest that students practice JQS facilitations immediately following a self-study course or workshop. Volunteers can be found everywhere. Work colleagues, family members, and friends are generally bountiful, and are great avenues to start accumulating practice hours. Once 80 hours are reached, practitioner status can be awarded at that time should the student desire it.

Do I or my client need to believe in JQS for it to work?

No. Neither the client nor the practitioner needs to believe in JQS for a healing facilitation. The rhythmic breathing technique the practitioner learns raises their bio-energetic vibration which is then absorbed into the client's bio-energetic field as healing Qi is sent. The client's body will continue to absorb the healing Qi until it matches the energetic frequency of the practitioner, triggering a healing response. This results from, and can be explained by, basic scientific principles.

Can JQS be combined with other healing arts?

Yes. I have known acupuncturists, chiropractors, physical therapists, massage professionals, cranial-sacral practitioners, and even Reiki practitioners who have combined JQS into their practices.

Can JQS be performed on children and animals?

Yes. JQS is safe for animals and children. I have found that animals and children respond quickly to healing Qi and will let you know when they have absorbed enough energy. I perform JQS on my pets regularly and they let me know when their session is over by moving away from my hands.

What is meant by facilitating a healing?

The JQS practitioner learns to be an energy conduit which directs healing Qi into the client. As such the practitioner does not actually heal the client; the Qi energy directed into the client's body heals the client. "Facilitating a Healing" is a term used by the JQS practitioner to stand in the gap for the client when they draw and send healing Qi.

What things does a client feel during a JQS session?

Healing Qi may manifest in the clients body in the form of heat, coolness, tingling, or as a prickly sensation. Sometimes the client may not feel anything at all. The client does not have to feel anything for healing to take place.

Is a JQS session ever painful?

Yes, sometimes it is. Once in a while a client may feel pain when they are receiving healing Qi. I tell my clients to breathe into the area they feel painful sensations and inform them that their body is responding to the healing Qi as it is being absorbed, and that healing is taking place. If a client experiences pain during a healing session continue to draw and send healing Qi until the pain has subsided.

Can I send too much energy?

No. The client's bio-energetic body will absorb only the healing Qi it needs to bring it back into harmony.

How many sessions does a client need?

I leave this up to my client. Chronic conditions (resulting from stagnant or condensed energy accumulated over a long period of time) may need additional attention, while acute conditions may need one or more sessions.

While facilitating a healing does the JQS practitioner deplete themselves of their own Qi?

No. As long as they JQS facilitator maintains the healing Qi breath throughout the healing facilitation they will not deplete themselves of their own Qi.

The Qi healing breath, whether or not performed in a healing environment, clears the mind and is quite invigorating. I always feel alert and energized after breath practice, and after a JQS facilitation.

Can you give suggestions on how to best facilitate a JQS session?

As a rule, always make the client as comfortable as possible. Other considerations, especially during Direct Qi Healing are to: keep the spine straight, be aware of your dantian, keep your tongue pressed against the upper palate, keep your Qi healing breath flowing continuously and smoothly throughout the facilitation, and put your ego aside. Let go of any expectations during the healing session. Hold a positive space for the client. Acknowledge your client's original essence which is a manifestation of All-That-Is. Surrender with love and trust and allow the healing response to manifest in your client.

Can I teach JQS to others?

I am often asked by students who have completed JQS training if they are able to teach the healing art to others. JQS is a Universal Healing Art. As such, we encourage students to teach the art to those who wish to learn it. For a deeper understanding of the art as a whole, it is suggested that the practitioner have 200 plus hours of healing facilitations prior to teaching the art to others. Teaching certification is available for those who wish it, but it is not necessary.

Jing-Qi-Shen, The Art of Universal Healing is a complete, comprehensive text which our certified instructors use during their teaching workshops. We encourage all instructors to provide their students a copy of the text as a teaching tool. If you wish to find out more about teaching certification, please contact us by e-mail and request additional information.

CHAPTER FOUR

QI BREATHING – HARNESSING UNIVERSAL HEALING ENERGY

Learning to harness the Universal Healing Energy is the most fundamental aspect of Jing-Qi-Shen (JQS). It is recommended that this chapter be studied thoroughly and that the energy sensitizing and breathing techniques be explored and practiced consistently, preferably on a daily basis, through out the student's course of instruction. The breathing techniques presented in this chapter are based on ancient Yogic and Chinese traditions which have been in existence for centuries.

The breath is considered sacred in many eastern spiritual practices, as well in many shamanic cultures. The breath is also very intimate as all mammals share in this vital elixir regardless of their unique species.

To function at optimum the cells of our body need oxygen. The respiratory system, which consists of air passages, pulmonary vessels, lungs, and diaphragm, supply fresh oxygen to the blood for distribution to the rest of the tissues and organs in the body. In addition, respiration removes carbon dioxide, a waste product extracted from the body processes.

The breath is one of the primary methods used in JQS to draw and direct healing energy. It takes twenty seconds for the blood in the body to circulate three times infusing fresh Qi to all the body cells. It would be prudent then to reason that good breathing habits can assist in maintaining great health.

All Asian and Yogic breathing traditions teach full breathing utilizing the diaphragm. Shallow breathing, that is breathing that centers in the chest, constricts the proper flow of Qi, or as Yogic traditions know it, prana throughout the body. This restricted air oxygen flow could result in diseases in the body such as hypertension, gastric conditions, ulcers, and many stress related disorders.

Exercise One. Basic Dantian Breathing.

The dantian is a qi energy reservoir located about two inches below the navel. It is also said to be the body's center of gravity. My own training in the Art of Jing-Qi-Shen stressed the importance of the dantian and the following breathing exercise was practiced extensively. This technique is a simple way to learn how to breathe through the diaphragm.

1. Sit or stand with the spine straight, hands placed lightly on the dantian, an area about two inches below the navel.
2. Breathe in deeply through the nose, allowing the air to expand the lower abdomen causing your hands to move slightly forward.

3. Next, exhale through your mouth, noticing your abdomen contracting and pulling in as you do so, and your hands moving slightly inward on the exhalation. Feel the air being exhaled in its entirety.
4. Slowly inhale through the nose once again and repeat the process with steps two and three. Continue the cycle for one to two minutes.

With all of the breathing practices presented in this chapter it is important to keep in mind these three things. These three things keep your body in energetic alignment and helps Qi energy to flow freely:

- Keep your spine erect. This not only allows the lungs and the diaphragm to fill fully, but also keeps the body in energetic alignment.
- Sink you hips (weight) down, "belly button" (naval) pointed up. You can imagine a heavy weight attached to each side of your hips.
- Keep your attention on the dantian.

Exercise Two. Full Body Qi Breathing, Part One.

In JQS, the Qi breathing technique is the foundation of drawing, building, and sending Qi healing energy. For the first part of this exercise we will concentrate on full body breathing and add the other components of this breathing technique in exercises to follow.

Full body Qi breathing draws earth energy up through the "yongquan", bubbling springs(foot chakra) points located on the soles of the feet, up through the legs and torso, and through the "baihui" point at the top of the head (crown chakra). The energy continues up about three inches over the head and then descends back down through the baihui, down through the neck (throat chakra) to the center of the chest (heart chakra); where it then splits off down each arm into the "laogong" points in the palm of the hands (hand chakras). We will discuss chakras in depth in an upcoming chapter.

I was taught that the reason the healing energy is drawn from the bottom of the feet to a place three inches over the head is to mix and cleanse the earth Qi with the Qi of Heaven. This is said to create a healing elixir comprised of purified subtle energy.

Throughout this exercise try to remember the points outlined at the beginning of the breathing exercises – spine strait, weight down, belly-button up, awareness on the dantian point. These all can be achieved easily if you just relax the body slightly (with belly-button pointing up) and feel as if your legs were weighted). Keep your tongue pressed against the upper palate. This creates a closed energy conduit inside the body. Inhalation of the breath is always done through the nose, and exhalation through the mouth.

1. Sit or stand comfortable with the spine erect. Become aware of the bubbling springs points on the soles of the feet. The bubbling springs point is also known as the foot chakra. The bubbling springs point can be located by curling your toes inwards. The small depression that is created in the center of the foot is the bubbling springs point. You can also just think of a point in the center of the sole of the feet. Lightly place one hand over the other leaving a small gap between the palms.
2. Imagine that each foot is resting gently on top of two fresh, bubbling wells of energy, whose energy source is located deep within the earth. Imagine the energy source entering up inside the soles of your feet, up inside both legs, up though your torso, and up above your head (baihui point)about three inches.
3. Exhale out through your mouth as you imagine sending the energy back down through the baihui point, down through the neck (throat chakra), to the center of the chest(heart chakra), where it then splits off down each arm into the "laogong" points in the palm of both hands(hand chakras).
4. Continue to perform full body Qi breathing for about five minutes for this exercise. Pay close attention to the sensations that begin to build up between your hands. You may experience tingling, heat, slight sweating, or a pulsating feeling in your hands. These are all good sensations and are normal. The sensations in your hands are an accumulation of healing Qi.

I can not over emphasis the importance of visualizing along with feeling or sensing the emerging moving up and down the body into the hands. In group and private JQS workshops I spend a considerable amount of time teaching the student techniques that quickly allow them to *feel* the energy moving. If you think that you can't feel anything, or if you have difficulty visualizing the energy moving, just pretend you can. By just relaxing and pretending that you can *see and feel* the energy moving, you will soon notice that you in fact do just that. There is an ancient Qigong saying, "Where the mind goes, Qi follows." I can still hear Xian Rinposhe's voice ringing in my ears, "Yi (mind) to Qi, Yi to Qi!"

Once you are comfortable with Part One of the full body Qi breathing technique, you can move on to Part Two.

Exercise Three. Full Body Qi Breathing, Part Two.

I've explained to you previously in Chapter Two that the body is an oscillating system, and discussed the process of rhythm entrainment. The Universal Healing Art of JQS teaches the facilitator rhythmic breathing as one of the primary methods of increasing his or her rate of vibration.

The JQS facilitator bases the rhythmic timing of the breath upon a unit corresponding with the heartbeat. This rhythmic breathing technique has been used by Yogi's for thousands of years, and through its practice they have been able to perform what seems like miraculous feats.

The heartbeat is individually unique and varies from person to person. It is therefore important to learn what the proper rhythmic standard is for you. To do this you will need to sit quietly and take your pulse. If you have never taken your pulse before it is a simple process. Look at your wrist. Generally there are two creases in you skin just underneath the palm of your hand. Place the thumb lightly on top of the second crease. You should now be able to feel a slight throbbing sensation. This sensation is your pulse. If you don't feel anything, vary the pressure on your thumb until you do.

After you have found your pulse, count the pulse beats: 1, 2, 3, 4, 5, 6; 1, 2, 3, 4, 5, 6; 1, 2, 3, 4, 5, 6; etc. in order to get the feel of the rhythmic count. The most important thing to acquire at this point is the mental idea of the rhythm of your own pulse. We are using six pulse beats to start with since most beginners usually complete a cycle of inhalation in about six pulse beats. As you practice you may notice that you may be able to increase this amount.

Let's apply this to the Full Body Qi Breathing technique. You would proceed exactly has described in exercise two; however the added component would be applying rhythmic breathing. While performing steps one through four in exercise two you would complete a cycle of inhalation for six pulse beats as you draw the energy up above the baihui point and ***retain it*** for three pulse beats. You would then exhale for a cycle of six pulse beats as you send the energy down into your hands, and once again retain the breath for three pulse beats. What we are doing is creating a specific rhythm which looks like this: inhale – 1, 2, 3, 4, 5, 6; retain – 1, 2, 3; exhale – 1, 2, 3, 4, 5, 6; retain – 1, 2, 3. The general rule for rhythmic breathing is that the units of inhalation and exhalation should remain the same, while the unit of the retained breath should be one-half of that of the number of inhale and exhale breath units.

As with any skill, practice makes perfect. Don't try to force your breath or your rhythm. Let it come naturally. The most important thing, once again is to get the feeling of the breathing rhythm that is natural for you.

The first time I practiced the complete Qi breathing technique I was amazed at how much healing Qi was being generated into my hands. My entire body felt a pleasant warm tingling running through it, and my hands literally felt as if they were buzzing.

You may notice when you practice that by varying the rhythm of your breath that you can increase the flow of the healing Qi into your hands. You will learn in subsequent chapters how to continually raise you energy vibration by coordinating your breath and other elements. The goal in facilitating healing Qi is to keep your own energy at an optimum beak. The full body Qi breathing technique in this chapter should be fully understood before proceeding on to the other exercises and practices presented in the instruction course.

Summary of Chapter:

- The Qi breathing technique is used in Jing-Qi-Shen to draw, build, and send healing energy.
- Proper breathing is done from the diaphragm.
- When performing the Qi breathing technique it is important to do the following:

  A) Keep the spine straight.
  B) Sink your weight down, bully-button pointed up.
  C) Be aware of your dantian point.
  D) Keep your tongue pressed up against the upper palate.
  E) Inhale through your nose, exhale through your mouth.

- The Universal Healing Art of JQS teaches the facilitator rhythmic breathing as one of the primary methods of increasing his or her rate of vibration.
- The JQS facilitator bases the rhythmic timing of the breath upon a unit corresponding with the heartbeat.
- The general rule for rhythmic breathing is that the units of inhalation and exhalation should remain the same, while the unit of the retained breath should be one-half of that of the number of inhale and exhale breath units.
- Practice, practice, practice.

CHAPTER FIVE

THE AURA AND THE ENERGY BODY

The following chapters will introduce you to the composition of the subtle energy body, beginning with the auric field in this chapter, and then moving on to the chakra system and the meridian system in subsequent chapters. Knowledge of the subtle energy body is important in JQS at it helps the healing facilitator to assess the overall health of the energy body, and to provide important clues to any imbalances that my reveal themselves during a diagnostic scan.

The JQS facilitator always begins and ends the healing session with work on the auric body. First there is a diagnostic scan of the auric body, followed by a general "brushing" of the auric layer, then concluding with an auric seal. This being the case, the study of the auric field is logically the first place to begin learning about one aspect of the subtle energy body.

What exactly is the aura? Ted Andrews, author of *How to See and Read the Aura* says the following, "Although defined in many ways, the aura is the energy field that surrounds all matter. Anything that has an atomic structure will have an aura, an energy field that surrounds it."

Every living thing has an aura, or energy filed, that surrounds its material body. In the human body, this energy field is a multi-layered, egg shaped, energy field surrounding the physical body. An average human aura will extend about 8 to 10 feet around the body. The higher the energy vibration in the body (both physically and spiritually) the larger the human aura extends out from around the physical body.

Thin, torn, or weakened auras shrink, or pull into the physical body. This reflects illness, or emotional or physical disturbances. The aura is also weakened by such things as drugs, alcohol, lack of exercise, poor diet, stress, lack of fresh air, and lack of proper rest.

Modern day science, along with its numerous documented studies have proven that aura's exist, and that they can be measured and recorded. The most revolutionary study on the human aura was done by Seymon Kirlian in 1939. Seymon Kirlian expanded on photography experiments using a high frequency, high voltage, electrical charge instead of light. Even though no actual light source was used, a border of light was captured around the circumference of the human model during this photographic technique.

The study of Kirlian Photography expanded with other experiments such a photograph of an energy healers hand during a healing session, photographs of a leaf freshly plucked from a tree (revealing a decreasing energy field around the leaf as the leaf dried out and the energy field around it decreased), and special photographs of people revealing various colors around the physical body, have helped to support the existence of a bio-energy field.

Auras can be pictured as a layered body within bodies. A great example would be like the layers of an onion. There are several individual layers found in the auric body. Beginning closest to the physical body and moving outward they are: the etheric layer, the emotional layer, the mental layer, the astral layer, the etheric template layer, the celestial body layer, and the ketheric template layer.

I am not going to describe each of these layers in detail as in JQS we are concerned primarily with the etheric layer. For a further in-depth discussion of these layers I would like to suggest Barbara Brennan's book *Hands of Light*, which I believe to be an excellent and informative book.

The etheric layer is the closest auric layer to the physical body, and is considered to be the energetic double of the physical body. Derived from the ancient Greek word "ether", meaning the place in the upper regions of the atmosphere (or heaven), the etheric layer acts as a bridge between the subtle energy body and the physical body.

The etheric layer is the easiest layer to learn to physically see with the eyes. It extends from the body about ¼ inch to 2 inches, and has a hazy bluish-white color. The following exercise will teach you to physically see the etheric layer, but in the healing art of JQS it is more important to sense the aura than to see it. So if you don't see it right away don't be discouraged.

Exercise Four. Learning to See the Etheric Layer.

This exercise can be performed on yourself, on a volunteer, on a pet (if they agree to cooperate), or a plant. You will need to find a white, black, or navy blue background of some sort. A sheet, towel, or oversized poster board in one of the above colors works beautifully. There are two variations for this exercise. I suggest you experiment with both variations.

Variation One.

1) Have your subject either sit or stand in front of a white, black or navy blue background. Note: If your subject is standing perform the exercise standing. If he or she is sitting, perform the exercise sitting.
2) With "soft" eye focus look at an area about two inches either above the top of the subject's head, or two inches above the shoulder/neck area. Do not focus on anything particular. Just let your eyes "blur out".
3) As you continue to sit with this relaxed focus you will eventually notice a thin white or bluish-white layer around the top of the head or shoulder/neck area. If you keep practicing eventually you will easily pick up on the bluish-white layer every time you do this exercise.

4) To perform this exercise on yourself find a mirror that enables you to view your head/shoulder/neck area with the appropriate colored background behind you. Then precede through steps two and three.

Variation Two.

1) Place your hand (fingers slightly apart) or your subjects hand over a white, black, or navy blue background.
2) With "soft" eye focus. Look at an area between the fingers. Don't focus on anything particular. Allow the eye to blur out.
3) Continue until you see a thin white or bluish-white light emanating around and between the fingers.

Tips:

As I indicated earlier, seeing the etheric layer in the practice of JQS is not as important as the ability to sense it. However, the preceding exercises give the practitioner a visual validation of his energy layer. When I was learning to see the etheric layer I became quite frustrated because I couldn't do it immediately. I expressed my frustration to Xian Rinposhe to which he replied, "You're trying too hard. Just do it Rinchen." His answered annoyed me at first. But eventually, I found that if I relaxed my desire to "see" right away and allowed myself to practice without expectation that I began to see this energy layer immediately.

Also, as has been the experience of many students, I first noticed a colorless energy wave around my subject, which then started to turn bluish-white the longer I held my gaze. This energy wave can best be described as the heat waves you might see coming off the barbeque grill or off hot asphalt.

Learning to Sense the Human Energy Field

Learning to sense the Human Energy Field, or auric field, is an important practice of JQS. Sensing the auric field enables the practitioner the ability to gather clues about the general state of the energy body. It is used as a diagnostic tool to help discover energy imbalances. These energetic imbalances reveal themselves as the sensation of hot, cold, stickiness, heaviness, prickly sensations, bumpiness, etc. They may also manifest as impressions of fear, sadness, nervousness, excitement, and the like. You will learn more about how to interpret the meaning of the impressions you receive as you progress through this course.

At this point, I would like to introduce you to some hand sensitizing exercises. This exercise, combined with Qi breathing, is an important basic fundamental in the healing art of JQS.

Your hands are the most important tool you posses as an energy healing facilitator. With your hands you learn to sense the energy body of your client, and also to send healing energy to your client. It is therefore advisable to practice these techniques as often as possible.

In Exercise Three, The Full Body Qi Breathing exercise, you learned how to draw Qi energy and send it to the laogong points (hand chakras) in the palm of your hands. The breathing exercise outlined in Exercise Three, demonstrates how the JQS practitioner draws and sends healing energy. If you practiced the full body Qi breathing technique correctly, you may have experienced one or more of the following sensations: tingling, heat, warmth, pulsing, etc. in your hands as you progressed through repetitions of the breathing pattern. For the next exercise you will perform full body Qi breathing with a simple added component which will aid you in learning to sense what the auric field feels like.

Exercise Five. Hand Sensitizing Exercise.

1) Perform the Full Body Qi Breathing technique as described in Exercise Three, with one palm held loosely over the other. Don't forget to keep your tongue pressed up against the upper palate. Begin the breathing technique for about two to three minutes. Feel the energy as it begins to build in your hands.
2) After a few minutes, allow yourself to return to regular breathing. Pull the palms of your hands gently apart about twelve inches, then slowly push them back towards one another, and then back again. The motion is like that of pushing and pulling on an accordion. See if you can sense a slight resistance between your palms. Workshop participants often describe sensations experienced during this exercise as that of sponginess, thickness, pillowy, cushiony, bounciness, balloon like, etc. I generally experience a squishy type sensation between my hands.

This exercise trains you to sensitize your hands. The squishy resistance (or what ever sensation you experience) is what it will feel like to you when you scan the auric body with your hands.

Although most of us are not aware of it, we already sense the auric field of others. Have you ever "sensed" that a particular person in a room is emotionally upset? There have been times when I have been out shopping when I was able to sense that someone, such as a sales clerk, was ill, angry, or sad. Their actions did not overtly display what I was sensing, yet I was able to feel imbalances emanating from their energy field.

When we sense someone's presence before we see them, sense that someone is looking at us, or experience situations where someone's presence either energizes us or drains us, we are sensing energy radiating from that persons auric field.

Exercise Six. Sensing Your Own Auric Field.

This next exercise will teach you to sense your own auric field.

1) Perform the full body Qi breathing technique for a few minutes, as you allow the energy to build up inside the hands.
2) Slowly lower your dominant hand (the hand you write with) towards the forearm of the opposite arm. Notice the sensations in you dominant hand. How close do you come to your forearm before you feel a slight resistance? Notice any sensations you experience in your hand, i.e. heat, tingling, thickness, etc.
3) Starting at the top of the forearm, near the elbow area, slowly move your hand along the slightly resistance energy field to the wrist. Notice any sensations you feel in your dominant hand. Notice any sensations you feel in your forearm as you slowly move your dominant hand down the forearm of the opposite hand to the wrist.

You have begun to learn to sense the subtle healing energy from your hands, and to feel your own auric layer. The next exercise will teach you how to sense the auric layer of another person. You will use this scanning technique at the beginning of every JQS healing session you facilitate.

Exercise Seven. Scanning the Auric Layer of Another Person.

You will need a piece of paper and a pen or pencil to write down your impressions after performing your scan. Your tongue should be pressed up against the upper palate throughout the entire exercise.

1) Perform full body Qi breathing for a minute or so. Feel the energy building inside your hands.
2) Stand facing your client. Shorter JQS practitioners may wish to stand on a small stepping stool if they can not reach their hands at least eight inches above their clients head.
3) Slowly move your palms in towards the crown of your partners head until you sense a change in the field between your hands and your partners head.
4) Moving your palms out to the side of your partners body, begin to trace the energy field passing the shoulders, moving down the side of the body, passing the hips, and down towards the ankles. Note any change in the pressure around the energy field. Do any of the areas you have passed your hands over seem to dip inwards? Did you sense any bumps in the energy field? Could any warm spots be sensed? Write down your impressions.
5) Repeat steps 3-4 scanning down the back of your partner's body. Record your impressions.

6) Repeat steps three and four scanning down the back of your partner's body. Record your impressions.

At JQS workshops I like to have students share their findings with their partners after this exercise. Beginning students are thrilled when the impressions they received during the scan of their partner's body are right on the money.

At one particular workshop a particular student demonstrated a need to know how to do everything right the first time she performed a particular exercise. As I walked about the room as the students practiced scanning their partners, I overheard this student berating herself for not being able to feel any sensations in her hands as she scanned her partner.

"Just pretend you can feel it," I told her. "Remember that where your mind goes, Qi follows." She agreed to try again, this time pretending that she could do it. She scanned her partner's body and then jotted down all her impressions.

When it came time for her to share with her partner what she felt during the auric scan she sarcastically said to her partner, "I *pretended* to feel heat around your lower abdomen, and then *pretended* to fell bumps in an area on both sides of your mid-back."

Much to her surprise, her partner began to laugh, then share that she was suffering from severe menstrual cramps that morning, and that she was diagnosed with a kidney infection just three days prior to the workshop.

Auric Brushing

Auric brushing is a technique used by the JQS practitioner in the beginning portion of the healing session. Its purpose is to clear the auric body of the dirty, stagnant energy. A clear aura allows the client to absorb healing Qi quicker. This in turn shortens the period of time it takes to affect a healing response.

A dirty, congested aura is like that of a murky, foul smelling, insect infested, well. A clean aura is like a well filled with crystal clear, sweet tasting water. Which would you rather drink?

There are two types of auric brushing techniques used in JQS. The first is full body brushing, and the second is local area brushing. Full body brushing removes stagnant energy from the entire auric body in general. Local area brushing is used to brush a specific area in the body that may be manifesting an energy blockage.

The JQS facilitator will always perform full body brushing during a healing session, and may also incorporate local area brushing if the situation calls for it. Local area brushing is also great when time constraints limit a complete JQS healing session.

Students have reported using local area brushing on friends, families, and even themselves for such things as headaches, sinus pressure, low back pain, swelling, and inflammation in the hands and wrists with quick relief. I have even used local area brushing on my pets with satisfactory results.

Exercise Eight. Full Body Brushing.

You will need a partner for this exercise. Have him or her stand facing you at a distance of about four feet. Read the exercise in its entirety before proceeding.

1) Perform full body Qi breathing for about a minute or too. Don't forget! Tongue on the upper palate. Keep it there during the entire exercise.
2) Move the sides of your hands together (palms facing towards the floor) by touching your index fingers and the inside edge of your hands together. Slightly curl your fingers so that they form a spoon or cuplike shape.
3) Raise both hands together (still touching) above your partners head, then smoothly bring them down, visualizing your hands as a super large, brilliant white, spoon sweeping down, over and through your clients head, down the center of his or her body, and through the legs and feet. Perform five more passes or repetitions as described above. Imagine the huge spoon scraping grey or muddy energy from the auric layers.
4) After performing the repetitions above, note any sensations in your hands. Do they feel sticky? Heavy? These feelings are due to the build up of dirty Qi on your hands. It is always advisable to sweep this stagnant energy off after three or four sweeping passes. Starting at the inside of your forearms, touch the palm of your opposite hand at the inside crease of the arm. Briskly sweep your palm down the inside of the forearm past the fingertips. Do this twice for each arm. Next, turn the palm of the arm being swept down ward and briskly sweep down from the top of the forearm at the elbow downward past the fingertips. This is also performed twice on each arm.
5) Perform Qi breathing again for another minute.
6) This time, with you hands spread apart about six inches (about the length of your partners shoulders) and the hands still slightly cupped, raise your hands above your partners head, and smoothly bring your hands down toward the feet. Imagine that your hands are two huge brilliant white spoons that go through your partner's body gathering grey or muddy energy as they move down your partner's body. Perform five more passes, and then sweep off your arms and hands as described in step number four.
7) Perform about one minute of Qi breathing again.
8) You will now extend your hands out twelve inches apart, and sweep down as described in step six for six passes, and then extend your hands apart twenty-four inches apart for six passes, and finally thirty-six inches apart, performing a totally of six passes. Make sure to sweep your arms and hands off after each third pass, and to perform about a minute of Qi breathing before starting a new set of brushing. Essentially what we are doing is

brushing the center line of our partner's body first, then extending our hands and brushing the sides of our partner's body, then the outer edges. This allows us to brush the entire auric body in four segments.

9) Have your partner turn with his or her back facing you, and perform the brushing technique as described above in each segment on the back aspect of the body.

Check in with your partner after performing the full body brushing technique. Ask them how they feel. Many of my clients and students tell me that they feel "lighter", cleaner, or relaxed.

Just Checking In:

How is your posture? Is your spine straight while performing each exercise? Is your weight sunk down, navel pointing up? Is your attention on your dantian? Is your tongue pressed against the upper palate?

Exercise Nine. Local Area Brushing.

Local area brushing is similar to full body brushing with the exception that only a local area of the body is energetically brushed.

You will need a partner for this exercise. If you are able to, try to find a partner that may be exhibiting pain or soreness in a localized area of the body.

1) Perform one to two minutes of Qi breathing. Scan the area of the body that is causing your partner discomfort and note what you sense – heat, coldness, thickness, etc.
2) Use one or two hands depending on the size of the part of the body being brushed. Slightly cup your hand(s) as you raise it/them up about two to three inches above the particular body part, and then briskly brush downwards over the area in a short pass (about two to three inches). Don't forget to visualize your hand(s) as a large, brilliant white spoon that is big enough to scoop through the entire body part. In your minds eye, visualize stagnant energy being gathered into the spoon. Perform about ten short, downward passes.
3) Sweep the energy off your arms and hands as described in step four of the previous exercise, perform a minute of Qi breathing, then repeat step number two again.
4) After sweeping the energy off your arms and hands, re-scan the body part seeing if you can sense any differences in the energy compared to your first scan. If you do not sense "clearness" in the area, or if you do not notice any change, repeat the entire exercise again.

Check in with your partner. Does he or she feel a difference in the area being brushed? Ask them to describe any differences or sensations that they may have experienced.

Summary of Chapter:

- The subtle energy body is important in JQS as it enables the facilitator to assess the overall health of the energy body, and provides important clues to possible physical imbalances and/or energetic disturbances.
- The aura is the energy field that surrounds all living matter. Modern science has scientifically verified that this energy field exists.
- The first auric layer, or the etheric layer, is the layer of the energy body that the JQS practitioner is primarily concerned with. The etheric layer acts as a bridge between the subtle energy body and the physical body.
- A clear aura allows the client to absorb healing Qi quicker, and shortens that time it takes to affect a healing response.
- It is more important to learn to "sense" the auric body than it is to learn to see it.

CHAPTER SIX

THE CHAKRA AND THE ENERGY BODY

Ancient Indian Yoga describes the main structure of the human energy body as six distinct centers called chakra. This also refers to different levels of consciousness and is often depicted as lotus flowers, or padmas. A seventh chakra above the head is also included, however, in Indian tradition it does not belong to the human body, but is related to the spiritual body.

In the previous chapter we have already discussed the auric layer which is the energetic field around all living beings. The chakra are important in the subtle energy body for various reasons. Much of the color in the auric field is supplied by the chakra. Where the auric layer acts as the bridge between the subtle energy body and the physical body, the chakras can be considered as the energetic processing station of the body.

"Chakrum" in the Sanskrit means "wheel". "Nadis" another Sanskrit word, refers to the subtle energy conduits or lines surrounding each one of us. The places where these nadis are produced and intersect are the chakra.

According to the teachings I received, there are seven major chakra in the human body, and thirty-two minor chakra. All of the chakra, major and minor, correspond to Chinese acupuncture points on the body. We will not discuss the minor chakra in this course as they are stimulated through work on the body's meridian system. There is an exception however in regards to the minor chakra located on both the hands and feet. These two sets of minor chakra are important in Jing-Qi-Shen as transmitters of healing energy. The minor chakra in the feet correspond to the Chinese acupuncture yongquan points (bubbling springs) and are responsible for drawing healing Qi from the earth. The minor chakra in the palm of the hands correspond to the Chinese acupuncture laogong points and are responsible for sending healing energy to the client. The hand chakra are also important for energy scanning of the client.

Viewed from a holistic standpoint these energy vortexes are responsible for receiving and processing life force energy, and in turn disseminating this energy to the mental, physical, and spiritual body. Blockages, or energetic dysfunctions in the chakra, result in deficient energy flows to certain portions of the body as well as an impairment in the entire energy field. This hinders the energy field's ability to process energy. Proper eating, thinking, physical rest, as well as proper energetic hygiene are therefore paramount to help the chakra function at optimal efficiency.

To really appreciate the importance of the seven major chakra and their relation in the healing environment (as well as the meridian system in the body), I recommend that you obtain a book on human anatomy and study the ten body systems paying careful attention to the nervous system and the endocrine system. There are thirty-one pairs of peripheral spinal nerves which emerge from the spinal cord and extend through spaces between the vertebrae. Each nerve divides and subdivides into a number of branches; two main divisions serve the anterior aspect and posterior aspect of the body in the region innervated by that particular nerve. Some of the branches of one spinal nerve will join with other nerves to form groups called plexuses; which innervate nerve ganglia and various organs through out the body. The nerve ganglia can be thought of as root bundles. These root bundles innervate, or provide signals, to every process in the body.

Physiologically, the seven major chakra are located near the seven major nerve ganglia which branch out from the spinal column. Each of the chakra also corresponds to glands in the endocrine system. The endocrine system is a collection of hormone-producing glands and cells located in various parts of the body such as the pancreas and testis. Hormones, made up of complex chemical substances, are secreted into the blood stream to assist and regulate various body functions.

The chakra also correlates with emotional and psychological components. These emotional and/or psychological symptoms reveal themselves during the initial scan of the chakra and also at times during a healing session. The facilitator should pay attention to any emotions they feel during a facilitation and make a mental note of the area of the body they are working on at the time it is experienced. In my experience, about 90% of emotions experienced during a healing facilitation are energy vibrations being picked up from the client. As energetic disturbances are released many times a client may cry, feel angry, feel sad, feel fearful, etc. I remind my clients that they are in a safe place and to not hold back tears or emerging feelings.

Jamie, a 26 year old accountant came for a healing session a few months after she had been promoted to a managerial position. Her promotion naturally bought with it increased job functions and responsibility. Jamie stated that shortly after her job promotion she began to feel a strange tightening sensation in the center of her upper stomach. Sometimes this tightness would cause her breathing to become shallow, and Jaime would notice that her stomach would become upset after eating. My scan of her solar plexus chakra wasn't too surprising. It felt small and closed in. As I continued to scan this area I began to experience a slight sensation of panic. When I began to work at clearing and rebalancing the solar plexus chakra Jamie told me that she felt as if she couldn't breathe. I had her take very slow, deliberate breaths. As she did so I explained to her that the solar plexus chakra is the center where negative energies related to thoughts and feelings are processed.

"Are you fearful or worried about something?" I asked her. Jamie began to cry. She felt overwhelmed with learning her new job duties along with learning how to balance her new responsibilities. She confided that she feared the possibility of failing in her new position. After the healing session was over I shared with Jamie some ideas that could possibly assist her with her situation at work. As was leaving my office she hugged me and stated, "Wow! I can totally breathe and that tight feeling is gone. Come to think of it, I feel at peace and feel really clear."

Characteristics of the Seven Major Chakra

Each chakra has its own assigned characteristics in the energetic body as well as the physical, mental and spiritual bodies. This includes its own specific color from the color spectrum, its own vibratory tone, and a host of other attributes. Knowledge of these characteristics will greatly enhance the effectiveness of your healing repertoire.

7th Chakra, Crown (Saharara):

Color: Violet to lilac, white, gold
Location: Crown of the head
Acupoint: Baihui (GV 20)
Body Organs: Muscular system, general skeletal system, skin, central nervous system, pituitary gland, cerebral cortex
Physical Disturbances: Depression, headaches, diseases of the muscular system, diseases of the skeletal system, skin disorders
Spiritual: Universal Oneness, return to the all, our connection to Divine Source
Sound or Mantra: Om (pron. 'ohm')
Harmonic Spectrum: Key of B, 480 Hz

6th Chakra, Third Eye (Ajna):

Color: Royal purple to indigo
Location: Between the eyebrows
Acupoint: Yintang
Body Organs: Pineal gland, eyes, ears, brain, hypothalamus, nervous system
Physical Disturbances: Eye or vision problems, ear problems, Parkinson's, Alzheimer's, brain disturbances, neurological disturbances, sinus problems
Spiritual: Intuition, telepathy, clairvoyance, truth vs. illusion
Sound or Mantra: Ham-Ke-Sian (pron. 'hahm-ksham')
Harmonic Spectrum: Key of A, 426.7 Hz

5th Chaka, Throat (Visuddha):

Color: Blue
Location: Throat
Acupoint: Tiantu (RN 22)
Body Organs: Throat, thyroid, parathyroid, neck, vocal cords, mouth, jaw, teeth, gums, ears, nose, trachea, tonsils

Physical Disturbances: TMJ, thyroid problems, hearing problems, sinus problems, sore throat, neck pain, tonsillitis, any disease in the mouth, teeth problems, gum disease
Spiritual: Artistic expression, clairvoyance, communication, surrender to Divine Truth
Sound or Mantra: Ham (pron. 'hahm')
Harmonic Spectrum: Key of G, 384 Hz

4th Chakra, Heart (Anahara):

Color: Green
Location: Heart
Acupoint: Zigong (RN 19)
Body Organs: Heart, circulatory system, lungs, thymus gland, diaphragm, shoulder, arms, hands, immune system, breasts, ribs, upper back
Physical Disturbances: Heart and cardiac disorders, problems with circulation, thymus problems, lung disease, asthma, bronchitis, arm and shoulder problems, upper back pain, disorders of the immune system, hypertension
Spiritual: Unconditional love
Sound or Mantra: Yam (pron. 'yahm')
Harmonic Spectrum: Key of F, 341 Hz

3rd Chakra, Solar Plexus (Manipura):

Color: Yellow
Location: Solar plexus, below diaphragm
Acupoint: Juque (RN 14)
Body Organs: Respiratory system, diaphragm, stomach, digestive system, small intestines, liver, gall bladder, kidney, pancreas, spleen, mid-spine, adrenal glens
Physical Disturbances: Digestive problems, gastric or duodenal ulcers, weight issues, hepatitis, diabetes, pancreatitis, adrenal dysfunction, gall stones, kidney problems, allergies, mid- spine pain (behind solar plexus to top of low back).
Spiritual: Aligning personal will with Universal will, realm of intellect, spiritual power
Sound or Mantra: Ram (pron. 'rahm')
Harmonic Spectrum: Key of E, 320 Hz

2nd Chakra, Naval (Svadisthana):

Color: Orange
Location: Underneath naval
Acupoint: Yinjiao (RN 7)
Body Organs: Large intestines, colon, sexual organs, lower vertebrae, bladder, appendix, lym-

phatic system, hip area, prostate, all bodily fluids
Physical Disturbances: chronic low back pain, pain in the hips, sexual dysfunction, female problems, arthritis, colitis, urinary problems, appendicitis, sciatica
Spiritual: To honor self and others, personal power, sexual union, physical survival
Sound or Mantra: Vam (pron. 'vahm')
Harmonic Spectrum: Key of D, 288 Hz

1st Chakra, Root (Muldahara):

Color: Red
Location: Base of spine, perineum
Acupoint: Huiyin (RN 1)
Body Organs: Base of spine, bones and bone marrow, immune system, legs, feet, rectum
Physical Disturbances: Chronic low back pain, sciatica, varicose veins, immune related disorders, depression, bowel problems, chronic fatigue
Spiritual: Connection to Source, physical survival, security, stability
Sound or Mantra: Lam (pron. 'lahm')
Harmonic Spectrum: Key of C, 256 Hz

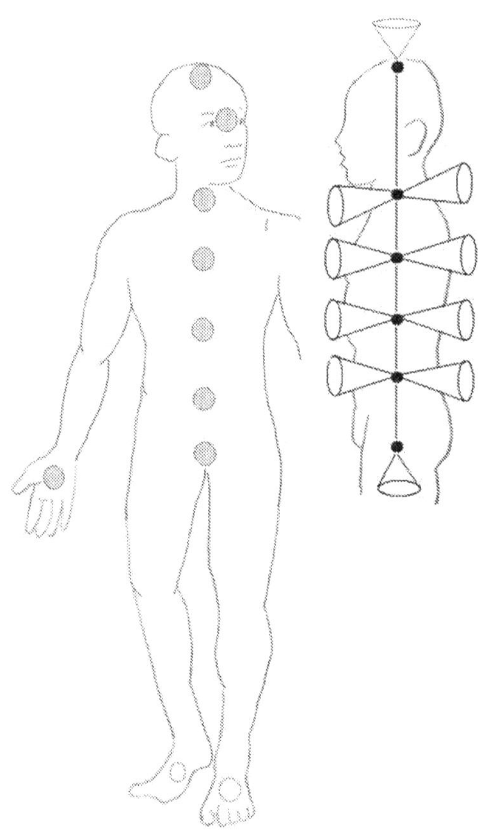

The Chakra System

Chakra Scanning and Testing

There are various methods that energy healing practitioners use to test the healthiness of the chakras. These methods may range from sensing the subtle energy of a specific chakra with the hands, the use of a pendulum, intuitive scanning, muscle testing, and a myriad of other techniques. I found that, depending on the skill of the energy healing practitioner has with the technique, that each of the above techniques can be effective. JQS utilizes hand scanning, muscle testing, and intuitive scanning in a combined two-step process.

Exercise Ten. Step One: Muscle Testing.

A very easy method for testing the overall basic health of the chakra system is the technique of muscle testing. Muscle testing is the practice of applying consistent force to a muscle in the body, then observing the response in the muscle being tested. Muscle testing, pioneered by Dr. John Goodhart in the year 1960, is a well known diagnostic tool of Applied Kinesiology. It is generally performed with the use of a specific stimulus. For the purposes of its use for testing the overall health of the chakra system, the stimulus is simply the client's awareness on the particular chakra being tested.

You will need a partner for Step One and Step Two of the following exercises.

1) Have the person to be tested stand in front of you with one of their arms extended straight out to their side at shoulder level.
2) Your partner should place their attention on the area of the chakra you will be testing. Have them tap the area a couple of times with their free hand. When testing the root chakra, instruct them to contract (pull in) the anal sphincter muscles a few time.
3) With the palm of one of your hands apply steady pressure on your partner's outstretched arm, instructing them to resist the pressure.
4) Repeat steps one through three until you have tested all seven major chakra. Make a note of the chakra which had strong resistance, and the chakra that had weak resistance.

When your partners arm has little or no resistance when testing a specific chakra, this is a signal that this chakra may be exhibiting either blocked or stagnant Qi energy, or excessive Qi energy, which would need to be cleansed and balanced.

Exercise Ten. Step Two. Chakra Scanning.

In the previous chapter you were given tools on how to scan the subtle energy of the auric field. The chakra scanning technique is very similar. The only difference is the added component of intuitive sensing. You may want to have a piece of paper and a writing utensil near by so that you can write down your impressions while they are still fresh in your mind.

Before you begin this exercise, give your partner permission to freely tell you any sensations, feelings, thoughts or visual images he or she might have while you scan each individual chakra. Your partner's input can help provide valuable insight into the issues pertaining to certain areas of the energetic, spiritual, and mental bodies. As with all of the previous exercises, remember to keep your spine straight, weight sunk down, and tongue pressed against the upper palate.

1) Have your partner sit or stand comfortably with legs or feet slightly apart, and their spine straight.
2) Activate your hand chakra by clapping your hands together a few times and briskly rubbing the palms of the hands together a few seconds.
3) Perform one to two minutes of Qi breathing.
4) Slowly move your hand in toward the root chakra, stopping when you feel the sensation of pressure, resistance, tingling, warmth or coldness. Sense the depth, width, and shape of the chakra.
5) In your minds eye (if it helps, close your eyes at this point in the exercise) notice the corresponding color the chakra. In this case, the color of a healthy root chakra is vibrant red. What did you "see"? For example, perhaps you perceived a dark red, muddy, or murky root chakra. This would signify "dirty" Qi. Did you intuitively see blotches of color? Brown, black, or white spots? Did you feel any strong emotional sensations such as sadness, anxiety, fear, joy, love? *Your first impressions are always the right impressions.* Record them. I call step five the "What do I intuitively see, sense with my hands, or feel?" step. If you are having difficulty with this step, "pretend" that you are "seeing", sensing with your hands, and are feeling. You are beginning to awaken your intuitive skills in this step. As with any skill, practice makes perfect. When I first began practicing the energy healing art of JQS I was only able to intuitively see spots and blotches of black or brown in the chakra I scanned. Yet, the subtle energy scan and the intuitive scan always provided me the information I needed in order to help facilitate healing energy to my client. Xian Rinposhe would always lovingly remind us to relax and to allow what ever impressions that come up, knowing that Divine Source would give us exactly what was needed to assist the client.
6) Ask your partner to share any sensations, feelings, thoughts or visual images they may have received while you were performing the scan. Record them.
7) Repeat steps one through six scanning the remaining six chakra.

This two step process, muscle testing and scanning should take less than 15 minutes to perform. If it taking longer than this you are over analyzing, which means you are trying too hard. Relax and receive.

An alternative practice to this two step chakra scanning technique used by many JQS facilitators is to perform the subtle energy scan and intuitive scanning process only on those chakra where muscle testing showed weakness. Some facilitators use both methods interchangeably. Utilize whatever method you feel particularly drawn to.

Interpreting the Chakra Scan

Quickly review the information you received from your scan. The information is helpful to you as the facilitator as it offers clues to areas where energy needs to be cleansed and balanced. Your chakra interpretation may simply be that of noticing that certain chakra are "dirty" or "spotty", small, or big.

To give you an idea about how to interpret your chakra scan, here is an example taken from a session with a client:

Dennis, a 46 year-old firefighter came to me with complaints of pain (resulting from a medical diagnosis of sciatica) in his right leg. The pain was severe enough that Dennis stated he would often loose his balance and stumble as he tried to walk. He was receiving acupuncture treatments at the time and was referred to me in order to help round out his treatment regimen.

My aura scan noted coldness, dips, and bumps in his low back, right buttock, right hip, and down his leg. Muscle testing of the 1st, 2nd, and 4th chakra provided barely any resistance as compared Dennis' strong unbendable arm with the remaining chakra.

My chakra scan of the 1st chakra revealed a small, closed in chakra that was almost brown in color. It didn't seem to be rotating. I kept hearing in my mind's ear "I can't seem to stay on my feet." During my scan, Dennis stated that he began to really long for his father who had passed away fifteen years earlier. The emotion was so strong that Dennis became uneasy.

As he began to open up more with me, Dennis revealed that he was newly divorced, had child support and spousal support to make, and that he was still responsible for the mortgage on the house where his children and ex-wife still resided.

I completed my scans and shared the following with Dennis: "The first chakra's function is survival, and it determines your grounding to earth energy. It has to do with security and stability. This chakra also has as one of its physical symptoms sciatica. Your root chakra was not clear, but appeared to me as muddy brown in color, and seemed small. As I scanned your root chakra I kept hearing "I can't seem to stay on my feet." Is perhaps your financial situation resulting from your divorce causing you to feel mentally, emotionally, and physically unbalanced?"

Dennis looked at me with an expression of surprise. He agreed with my assessment and as he did he had an instant knowing of why he had suddenly yearned for father.

"I just realized that my Dad was always my strongest advocate. I guess I have just been looking for someone to lean on."

After presenting my findings of the other chakra, I was better prepared to coordinate and facilitate an effective healing.

It is worth noting that energy blocks in the chakra system are each individual's responsibility because they are often times self-induced and not a result of natural environmental factors. The JQS facilitator's task is to show clients how they may have blocked their system, so that their clients can then begin to understand how their physical condition or illness may have occurred.

Cleansing and Balancing the Chakra

After scanning, the JQS facilitator will always clear (cleanse) and balance the chakra before facilitating a direct healing. I recommend that students cleanse and balance their chakra on a daily basis in order to keep their energy vibration humming at optimum.

Exercise Eleven. How to Cleanse The Chakra.

The following method can be used for clearing your own chakra or those of your client. You will need a partner for this exercise. Your partner may sit or stand.

1) Start from the root chakra and work your way up. Place one hand over the root chakra (about two inches above the area). Move your hand counter clockwise for about five to ten rotations. As you do this, imagine that your hand is a giant spoon or soup ladle. Still moving counterclockwise, visualize the spoon or ladle scraping out and gathering all stagnant, dirty Qi energy until the chakra looks clean and clear in your minds eye, and is radiating in its true vibrant color.
2) Perform two to three sets of five to six rotations on each chakra making sure to sweep any Qi build up off your hands between each step.

Exercise Twelve. Balancing.

After all the chakra have been cleared its time to rebalance them. The following technique balances not only the major chakra in the body, but also two Qi meridians in the body. The front and rear aspect of the seven major chakra are positioned along these two important meridians. The Du Mai or Governing meridian is the super highway of yang Qi in the body. It begins at the base of the perineum, runs up the spine, over the crown, ending at the upper lip. The Ren Mai or Conceptual meridian is the super highway of yin Qi in the body. It begins underneath the bottom of the lower lip and runs in a straight line down the middle of the body to the perineum.

1) Your client will be seated in a chair or stool for this procedure. Stand beside him or her and begin Qi breathing. You will be performing Qi breathing through out the entire balancing procedure.
2) Verbally set your intention. For example, "It is my desire to rebalance and align the seven major chakra." Or, "I now rebalance and align the seven major chakra."
3) Place your hands about four inches above the crown chakra. Visualize a brilliant white beam of white light coming down from the heavens and entering the center of the crown chakra, moving down the center of the body where it descends for miles into the earth. As you do this, allow pure white healing Qi (generated from your Qi breathing) to flow from your hands into the crown chakra.
4) Slowly move your hands down, palms facing inwards until one hand is positioned about four inches over the third eye chakra, and one hand about four inches at the back of the head. Continue to allow pure white healing Qi to flow from your hands into the third eye chakra.
5) Slowly move your hands down, until one hand is positioned about four inches over the throat chakra, and one hand about four inches behind the neck. Continue to allow pure white healing Qi to flow from your hands into the throat chakra.
6) Slowly move your hands down once again until one hand is positioned about four inches in front of the heart chakra, and one hand is about four inches directly behind the heart (at the area between the shoulder blades). Continue to allow pure white healing Qi to flow from your hands into the heart chakra.
7) Proceed as indicated above throughout the remaining chakra with hand positions as follows: Continue to slowly move your hands down with one hand in front of the solar plexus chakra, and one hand directly behind it (at the middle of the back), one hand in front of the navel chakra, and one hand directly behind it (at small of the back), and finally one hand directly in front of the genitals and one hand directly behind (over the anus). Continue to allow pure white healing Qi to flow from your hands as you balance each remaining chakra.
8) Sweep off your arms and hands when you are finished.

Summary of Chapter:

- There are seven major chakra on the human body, and thirty-two minor chakra according to JQS teachings.
- The chakra are considered the energy processing stations in the body. They are responsible for receiving and processing life force energy, and in turn disseminating this energy to the mental, spiritual and physical body.

- There are two sets of chakra in the hands and in the feet which are important in JQS. The feet chakra assist in drawing up healing Qi from the earth, and the hand chakra assist in sending healing Qi into the client.
- Physiologically, the seven major chakra are located near the major nerve ganglia which branch out from the spinal column.
- The seven major chakra correspond to, and help to, regulate the endocrine system in the body.
- Blocks or energetic dysfunctions in the chakra results in deficient energy flows to certain portions of the body, as well as impairment in the energetic field.
- Each chakra has its own assigned characteristics in the energetic, physical, and spiritual bodies. Knowledge of these characteristics are beneficial to the JQS practitioner in order to effectively facilitate a healing.
- Muscle testing and chakra scanning are methods used in JQS to help test the healthiness of a chakra. The information received provides the facilitator information on areas of the body where Qi energy needs to be cleansed and balanced.
- The JQS facilitator will always cleanse and balance the chakra before facilitating a direct healing.

CHAPTER SEVEN

INTUITION AND THE PERCEPTIVE ANALYSIS

As you have discovered from the previous chapters, the Universal Healing Art of Jing-Qi-Shen trains the facilitator to develop a keen ability to sense subtle energy, and provides the facilitator an effective means on drawing and sending healing Qi into the client. Another very potent and fascinating skill JQS provides to the healing facilitator's "tool belt" is that of intuition.

By its very nature, JQS is an intuitive healing art. Through age old breathing techniques the healing facilitator is taught techniques on how to still the mind so that he or she can "look" inside the body at the bones, organs, and diseased sights.

This is accomplished by three scanning techniques that are performed prior to the direct healing session. These techniques are the Auric Scan, the Chakra Scan, and the Perceptive Assessment. The Auric Scanning technique and the Chakra Scanning technique were presented in Chapters Five and Six. The Auric and Chakra Scans assists the facilitator in assessing the etheric body (aura) and its specific stations (the chakra). The Perceptive Scan, presented in a later section of this chapter, allows the facilitator to intuitively look inside the major organs in the client's body to detect possible energy deficiencies.

Intuition is a latent ability in all human beings. It generally manifests itself as a flash of knowledge or insight that provides instant illumination. It is not some mysterious, mystical process by which one use tarot cards, crystal balls, or conjures up spirits (although for some people these are effective tools that help tune into "The Knowing"; but they do not have a place in JQS). You do not *become* intuitive. You *are* intuitive. Intuition is about learning to sense or tune into the energy vibrations around you.

How can one learn to tune into these energy vibrations? The Universal Healing Art of JQS teaches three basic principles that help facilitators to tap into a pool of intuitive knowing in order to help to bring a client back his or her original state of wholeness. These three principles are: asking, receptivity, and trust. Longtime JQS facilitators regularly inform me that they notice a significant increase in intuitive abilities the more they facilitate healings. They report that the increase in intuitive abilities carry over into everyday living.

The three principles are applicable and useful to situations outside the healing environment as well as within, but my elaboration will be directed at their use during a healing facilitation.

Principle Number One: Asking

The first principle is that of asking. Tibetan teacher Sogyal Rinpoche, author of the *The Tibetan Book of Living and Dying,* writes "All we need to do to receive direct help is to ask. Didn't Christ also say: "Ask and it shall be given you; seek and ye shall find; knock and it shall be opened unto you. Everyone that asketh receiveth; and he that seeketh, findeth"? And yet asking is what we find hardest. Many of us, I feel, hardly know how to ask."

A child leans early in his or her life to ask for what they need. As infants they cry if they are thirsty, hungry, or soiled. As they mature they begin to learn to verbalize their needs and wants. We live in an ever expanding Universe in which the Law of Asking can not be restricted. We can, like Aladdin and his magic lamp, ask for anything we desire as long as it doesn't infringe upon the rights of others.

The JQS facilitator is a being in awakening. As such, the awareness of a Supreme, All Knowing, Infinite Source is generally heightened. It does not matter what you wish to call this Divine Source – Buddha, Krishna, Jesus, The Tao, the Higher Self – they are all part of the same Spiritual Essence.

Asking is not about pleading. Jesus never advocated begging. "*Ask* and you shall receive", states Christian scripture. This asking is one of coming boldly, with confidence, before whomever you call your Infinite Source.

In a healing environment the JQS facilitator *asks* to be shown something, or *asks* for specific clarification or knowledge of something particular. For example, you may be doing a scan of the chakra system and ask to be shown the second chakra, "Show me the second chakra." Or you may be performing a perceptive assessment and ask, "Show me the liver."

Your asking may also consist of gleaning additional information. Perhaps during one of your scans you perceive some shades of grey on the liver. You could request additional information by asking Infinite Source to, "Give me more information about these grey areas."

To elaborate, the lumps, bumps, cold or heat spots you sense during your initial scans of the etheric and internal bodies are all signifies of a block in that particular area. When you scan the chakra, aura, or physical body intuitively you are able to use the clues you intuitively receive on either a physical or energetic disturbance, to ask Divine Source for additional intuitive insight if needed.

The Law of the Universe is to always give us what we ask for, which brings us to principle number two, receptivity.

Principle Number Two: Receptivity

Receptivity is a state of being in which you are open to receive that which you have asked for. It is the process of being open to the inner guidance of your soul.

Intuitive impressions in a healing facilitation come in varying forms. The JQS practitioner learns to distinguish and to listen to each of these variations. The answer to your asking may come (or be *received)* in the form of images symbols, sounds, feelings, a sudden clear "knowing", or in a combination of the above.

Many times our intuitive knowing speaks to us in symbols and metaphors. The following story is a great example of an intuitive impression received via a metaphorical representation. A family member called me on the telephone and during the course of our conversation complained of pain in his lower abdomen. After I hung up the telephone I asked Source to show me the nature of this pain. Immediately, in my minds eye, I saw my relative laying on top of an examination table as man with chopsticks was eating noodles from his lower abdomen. This intuitive impression surprised me and did not seem to make any sense so I then asked, "Tell me what this image means." I suddenly had an instant knowing of the problem at which time the word "hernia" popped into my mind. This was later confirmed by his physician and repaired via surgery.

Intuitive symbolism is also a common way to receive impressions. Intuitive symbols are different for each healing facilitator. One may intuitively see bubbles in the stomach area and perceive it to be gas or indigestion. Another facilitator may see bubbles and perceive something entirely different. I intuitively see cancer as dark sticky blobs, while one of my healing teachers perceives cancer as a layer of thick, black tar.

At JQS healing seminars I am almost always asked if it is necessary to know all the disorders and diseases in the body. I answer this question with a yes and a no. The more you are aware of diseases and disorders and their pathology, the easier it will be for Source to provide you with a clearer intuitive picture or idea concerning the energy deficiency being manifested in the body. However, regardless of whether or not you know the exact pathology of the energy block you are sensing; you can have utmost faith that the energetic curiosities gleaned by your scans is sufficient to determine that erratic energy exists and that it needs to be cleared.

I suggest that all JQS healing facilitators keep a journal or notebook to record the things they intuitively perceive during their scans. Not only does this practice bolster confidence, but it also provides the facilitator with a reference of personal intuitive symbols which can be built upon. The personal reference book allows the practitioner to glimpse what I call "intuitive speak", which is a personal record of how one's intuitive voice speaks to them.

The intuitive voice may communicate with emotions, sounds, and even smells. Pay attention to every signal you receive. *Always trust your impressions. Never second guess them. You are not making them up.* This leads us to principle number three, trust.

Principle Number Three: Trust

Trusting your intuitive voice in an act of faith in Divine Source. It is the ability to let go and let your Spiritual Source initiate a healing response according to Universal Law. It is crucial to remember that all illness or disease in the body is a result of condensed energy. The facilitator is the person who stands in the gap for their client to assist in releasing and clearing the solidified energy pattern. This being the case, *the JQS facilitator does not actually heal anyone.* The client is the healer. As a healing facilitator our trust should be in the client's innate ability to receive the energy we are sending so that the client's body can heal itself. The facilitator scans the energy bodies, clears stagnant energy, and raises the client's vibratory rate by drawing and sending energy. That's it.

The more the JQS practitioner facilitates healings the more trust and confidence will be built up. This is where your journal of recorded client sessions becomes valuable.

How do I know if my intuitive impressions are correct? I am asked this question without exception at every JQS workshop I teach. My answer is that I know that my perceptions are always accurate because I come forth and ask in love for the good of my client. When I come in a spirit of love and an attitude of "show me what I can do to help", the still small voice of the Divine is very clear. When a practitioner comes forth in the power of their own ego, thinking that they are doing all the work and causing healing, the voice of the Divine is muted, and sometimes drowned out all together. If we can come from a place of love we can know without a doubt that what we perceive is accurate. We only doubt when our ego is screaming for recognition.

The process of trust is lovingly letting go of our own conscious agenda during a healing facilitation. In her book *The Lightworkers Way*, Doreen Virtue says: "We can't force a healing to occur; we can only forcefully hold the knowingness of Divine Truth within our hearts and mind. Then we must let go of attachment to the outcome and allow God's Law of Love to affect its natural course."

The Psychic Component of Qi Breathing

We can not overlook the incredible power of Qi breathing in relation of intuitive perception. The full body Qi breathing technique is based on ancient yogic teachings. Its ability to open up the gateway to intuition has been documented in yogic texts for centuries.

You have already learned that the rhythmic healing breath enables the facilitator to increase his or her energy vibration to optimum in order to raise the client's energy vibration and causing it to match that of the practitioner through the process of entrainment.

Rhythmic breathing relaxes the mind and body allowing a receptive state of being during a healing facilitation. Rhythmic breathing also alters the brain waves allowing the facilitator to slip into alpha or theta. There are four basic brainwave patterns: beta, alpha, theta, and delta. Experiments with healers have shown that the brain slips into alpha or theta during a healing session, so that will be our main focus. The alpha and theta brainwave patterns have been shown to correlate with psychic experiments and healing energy. The alpha range of brain activities occurs at 8 to 12 cycles per second. The theta range of brain activity occurs at 4 to 8 cycles per second.

In 1929, Austrian psychiatrist Hans Berger was the first to record EEG brainwaves in humans. Through his various studies he found that when a person's eyes were closed that the brain automatically started generating regular waves around 8 to 12 cycles per second (alpha). I find this fascinating and quite comforting as a JQS practitioner since the majority of my healing work is done with my eyes closed.

The Perceptive Assessment

The perceptive assessment is the last of the scanning techniques in the JQS practitioner's tool-kit. The auric and chakra scans help to assess the client's energy on an etheric level. The perceptive assessment intuitively scans the organs inside the body in order to provide the JQS facilitator with a snapshot of the energetic quality inside a particular organ or bone.

As in the chakra and auric scans, the facilitator will scan for the quality of Qi energy being sensed in a particular organ (i.e. hot, cold, squishy, stuck, hard, superficial, slow, fast, etc.), and record any intuitive impressions that may come in the form of intuitive impressions, metal pictures, symbols, or metaphors. For example, one may intuitively perceive a black or brown mist in or on an organ, dark spots, bumps, depressions or dips, etc. Or, metaphorically, you may intuitively perceive an organ being carried by a withering, weak old man (indicating a weakening organ perhaps), or an organ that is shaped like a feather bed mattress (indicating that the organ is not strong). Consistent with the other scanning techniques, the impressions received during the perceptive assessment are clues or indicators of energy deficiencies inside the organ being scanned.

Exercise Thirteen: The Perceptive Assessment.

The twelve major meridians in the body begin and end at either a finger or a toe. The perceptive assessment uses these points as an intuitive link to the organs that each meridian represents. You may wish to consult an anatomy chart before beginning this exercise.

Preparation: Your client should be either sitting on a stool or on the edge of a massage table. They may also lay face up on the floor or massage table. The client's shoes and socks should be removed.

This is an optional suggestion, but I like to have my clients wash their hands and feet with either a moist towelette I provide them with, or with a couple of squirts of antibacterial gel. Germs and bacteria tend to accumulate on the hands and feet so cleansing the hands and feet benefits not only the client, but the facilitator as well.

Your tongue should be pressed against the upper palate during the entire assessment.

1) Activate your hand chakras by clapping your hands together a few times and then briskly rubbing them together.
2) Perform 1-2 minutes of full body Qi breathing.
3) Take your client's thumb and lightly hold the tip between your thumb and forefinger. You will perform this assessment on the fingers and thumb of the left hand if your client is a man and on the thumb and fingers of the right hand if your client is a woman. Your free hand should be held over the corresponding organ, which in this case are the client's lungs. Intuitively "look" into the client's lungs as you slowly pass your free hand over the area noting any sensations of hot, cold, happy, sad, sticky, mushy, etc. Are the lungs clear, cloudy, spotty, dark, etc.? Make a note of what you perceive.
4) Perform two cycles of full body Qi breathing between each finger and toe. Continue as in steps two through three for all the remaining fingers and toes following the finger and toe correspondence listed below. You will hold the toes of the left foot if your client is a man, and the right foot if your client is a woman.

Hand

Thumb: Lungs
Index Finger: Large Intestine
Middle Finger: Pericardium and Reproductive Center
Ring Finger: Triple Warmer. For this meridian you will just assess the energy pulsation in the meridian.
Little Finger: Heart and Small Intestine

<u>**Foot**</u>

Big Toe: Spleen and Liver
Second Toe: Stomach
Third Toe: Circulatory System (Not used in perceptive assessment)
Fourth Toe: Gall Bladder
Little Toe: Bladder
Yongquan (Bubbling Well) Acupoint: This acupoint corresponds to the kidneys. To find the yongquan point on your client have him or her contract the toes backwards or forwards. You will notice a slight dip or depression in the foot about a third of the way from the toes to the heel. Place your thumb lightly on this area and hold the top of the foot with your fingers (your client can relax their toes!). Since the kidneys are located on the posterior side of the body it helps to have your client bend his or her knee and rest their foot on top of the massage table or chair. This allows the facilitator to easily reach the scanning hand behind the client's body to scan the kidneys.

The perceptive assessment is the final of the three energy scans that the JQS practitioner uses to determine the Qi energy of the aura, chakra, and internal organs. Once you have a basic roadmap of the energy workings inside your clients body you are ready to go on to the next step in your healing facilitation which is clearing blockages and treating the Qi dysfunctions indicated by your assessment.

Part of your treatment regimen is to work on clearing the energy pathways in the body called meridians. A detailed explanation of the meridian system is presented in the following chapter.

Summary of Chapter:

- Intuition is a latent ability all human beings possess.
- Intuition is about learning to sense or tune into the energy vibrations around you.
- The three principles of intuition are: Asking, Receptivity, and Trust.
- Asking is the process in which the JQS facilitator asks Divine Source to "be shown" or for knowledge about something particular.
- Receptivity is a state of being open to receive that which you have asked for. It is the process of being open to the inner guidance of your soul.
- The answers to your asking are received in the form of images, symbols, metaphors, sounds, feelings, a sudden clear *knowing*, or in a combination of all the above.
- Trust is the ability to "let go and let God" initiate the healing response in your client.
- The healing facilitator's trust must also be in the client's innate ability to receive healing energy so the body can heal itself.

- The rhythmic Qi healing breath used during a healing facilitation automatically slows the brainwaves of the practitioner to that of alpha or theta. Both alpha and theta brainwaves have been measured by the use of an EEG machine and have been found to correlate with both psychic experiences, and healing energy.
- The perceptive assessment is an intuitive scan of the organs or bones of the client in order to provide the JQS facilitator with a snapshot of their energetic quality.

CHAPTER EIGHT

THE MERIDIAN SYSTEM

The meridian system theory is of major importance in Traditional Chinese Medicine. "Theory" is used to describe an established explanation of what the meridian system is and how it is used. Traditional Chinese Medicine has existed for thousands of years before the development of conventional western medicine. In fact, according to historical evidence, Chinese physicians were performing sophisticated surgeries many years before the birth of Christ.

Many studies of Chinese medicine within the last fifty years have proven its effectiveness. One of these studies was conducted in 1960 by a group of Soviet physicians. The Soviet study verified the existence of meridians and energy points at the precise locations on the body as mapped out by Chinese physicians centuries ago.

The meridian system is a network of subtle energy flow inside the body. The energy of these meridians course deep inside the body and are normally inaccessible to direct touch. However, there are points on the skin along the energy path where the energy flow can be accessed with a finger or an acupuncture needle. These points are called "Xue" or energy points and are used in acupuncture, acupressure, and Chinese massage modalities.

The energy flow in the meridians can also be accessed and directed through the use of subtle energy, such as the subtle energy the JQS practitioner generates through Qi breathing. The Qi breathing technique along with the manipulation of the most important Xue points is an important practice in the healing art of JQS. We will discuss the Xue points further in an upcoming portion of this chapter.

The meridians are classified into two main groups: primary and secondary. Primary meridians flow directly to major internal organs while secondary meridians do not. The meridian system can continue to be broken down into even smaller components such as meridian extensions, muscle-meridians, collaterals, and sub-collaterals. However, the focus of the JQS practitioner is solely on the primary meridians along with two important secondary meridians.

There are twelve primary meridians each of which are named for their specific relationship to the organ they represent, and how the organ processes energy.

The Yin "Zang" organs are the heart, spleen, liver, lungs, and kidneys. The Yin Zang organs are responsible for storing energy.

The Yang "Fu" organs are the gallbladder, stomach, small intestine, large intestine, bladder, colon and Triple Warmer. The yang fu organs are those organs that transform food and drink into energy and eliminate that which is not needed through bodily processes.

The primary meridians are in pairs and are arranged symmetrically in the body. This means that there are actually twenty four primary meridians, but for convenience only one pair will be described.

The Twelve Primary Meridians.

The following list describes the twelve primary meridians along with their respective functions inside the human body. The illustrations (found in Appendix C) also list the important Xue energy points, along with its corresponding acupuncture point. I will not be describing the individual characteristic of each Xue point as I believe the overall description of the particular meridian's function along with the disorders associated with any blockages are sufficient. If you would like to find out specific details of any of the Xue points listed please consult an acupuncture reference book. The extra effort expended for the knowledge you may glean is well worth it.

Lung Meridian

The lungs are a part of the respiratory system. They distribute fresh oxygen to the blood for distribution to the rest of the body tissues. Through the process of respiration the lungs also assist with the removal of carbon dioxide which is a waste product from the body processes.

The Lung Meridian begins just under the opposite lung (just underneath the lowest rib), moves up the center of the chest to the throat area, and then down beneath the collar bone along the inner arm to the thumb.

Diseases and disorders associated with the Lung Meridian are: Respiratory diseases, bronchitis, pleurisy, pneumonia, swollen and/or sore throat, cough, shortness of breath, pain in chest, fever, common cold, flu, chest fullness, acid based (alkaline) imbalances, wrist pain, thumb stiffness or pain, pain in the shoulder and along meridian path.

Large Intestine/Colon Meridian

The large intestine absorbs most of the remaining water from digested food, converts the remaining matter into feces, where it is then sent to the colon for excretion.

The Large Intestine/Colon Meridian starts at the tip of the index finger and runs up the out side of the arm along the forearm, moving over the shoulder to the side of the neck, to the upper lip, and over the upper lip ending at the side of the opposite nostril.

Diseases and disorders associated with the Large Intestine/Colon Meridian are: Swollen face, hearing difficulty, headache, abdominal pain, constipation, diarrhea, vomiting, swollen and/or sore throat, toothache in the lower gum, herpes simplex on lips, nasal discharge, nasal bleeding, pain in hamstring, pain in the forearm, wrist, elbow, or along meridian path.

Stomach Meridian

The stomach receives liquids and chewed food at which point it churns, digests, and stores food preparing to enter the rest of the digestive processes in the body.

The Stomach Meridian begins underneath the middle of the eye where it moves down just underneath the cheek bone, moving side ways to the jaw bone, straight up about three finger widths above the end of the eyebrow, over about three finger widths above the beginning of the eye brow, straight down passing the inner eye, side of the nose, upper and lower lips, down the chin, down beside the throat, over across the top of the mid-point of the collar bone, straight down past the nipple, down beside the midline of the torso to the skin crease in the leg, then down the front of the leg ending at the tip of the second toe.

Diseases and disorders associated with the Stomach Meridian are: Stomach problems, gastritis, indigestion, abdominal pain, abdominal distension, constipation, colitis, edema, vomiting, sore throat, facial paralysis, upper gum toothache, teeth grinding, esophagus disorders, diaphragm disorders, acne, blurred vision, redness and swelling of eye, asthma, chronic fatigue syndrome, fibromyalgia, ovary dysfunctions, appendicitis, diabetes, gallstones, pancreatitis, hypo/hyperglycemia, acid based (alkaline) imbalances, peptic ulcer, Crohn's disease, cirrhosis, kidney or adrenal glad dysfunctions, neck pain, knee pain, shin splints, shin pain, aches and pain along meridian path.

Spleen Meridian

The spleen is one of the largest of the lymph organs. It assists the immune system by producing antibodies and filtering out damaged red blood cells.

Beginning at the tip of the big toe, the Spleen Meridian flows up the inner side of the leg, up the midline of the torso to the crease of the armpit, and ends at the second rib under the arm pit.

Diseases and disorders associated with the Spleen Meridian are: Problems of the spleen and pancreas, indigestion, diarrhea, vomiting, bowel problems, abdominal distension, constipation, uterine bleeding, uterine fibroids, endometriosis, fallopian tube dysfunctions, menstrual abnormalities, thyroid problems, prostate problems, heart palpitations, diabetes mellitus, thigh pain, medial aspect knee pain, pain in the latissimus dorsi muscles, pain in the triceps muscle, trapezius muscle pain, pain and/or stiffness of the big toe, pain along meridian path.

Heart Meridian

The heart is the body's blood pumping station. It pumps blood through the arteries, veins, and smaller vessels.

The Heart Meridian begins at the crease of the armpit and flows down the side of the inner arm ending at the tip of the little finger.

Diseases and disorders associated with the Heart Meridian are: Heart problems, angina pectoris, chest pains, heart palpitations, numbness, pain or stiffness of the hand and arm, pain in armpits, wrist pain, pain or stiffness in the little finger, dryness of the throat, stiffness in tongue, stuttering, retinal hemorrhages, insomnia, sleep apnea, pain along meridian path.

Small Intestine Meridian

The small intestine is comprised of three sections, each of which produces a digestive enzyme which contributes to the breakdown and absorption of food.

The Small Intestine Meridian begins at the lateral side of the tip of the little finger, extends up the outer side of the arm up to the back of the shoulder, crosses the scapula, extends up the side of the neck to the cheekbone, then extends back to the entrance of the middle of the ear.

Diseases and disorders associated with the Small Intestine Meridian are: Lower abdominal pain, diarrhea, colitis, blurred vision, swollen and sore throat, swelling or paralysis of face, swollen lymph nodes in cervical neck region, heart disorders, tinnitus, deafness, ear disorders, hand and wrist pain, stiff neck, headache, shoulder, arm, elbow pain, TMJ, toothache, quadriceps weakness or pain, pain along the meridian path.

Urinary Bladder Meridian

Waste products filtered from the blood by the kidneys are excreted in urine which passes through the urinary system to the bladder where it is stored until it can be expelled from the body through the urethra.

This meridian begins at the inner corner of the eye and goes over the head to down the side of the cervical spine to the occipital ridge. At this point the meridian splits into two parts.

From the occipital ridge it descends down the side of the spine to the buttock, and continues down the back of the leg below the outer ankle bone, continues along the side of the foot and ends at the tip of the little toe.

The second part of the meridian begins to the side of the occipital ridge and descends down across the scapula and goes down the back in a straight line passing the buttock, the back of the leg, below the outer ankle bone, along the side of the foot, ending at the tip of the little toe.

Diseases and disorders associated with the Bladder Meridian are: Bladder and kidney problems, urinary frequency, painful urination, chronic cystitis, headache, swollen eyes, blurred vision, vision disorders, loss of hearing, ear disorders, headaches, stiff or painful neck, cervical curving, abdominal pain, shoulder and back pain, chest pain, hypo/hypertension, jaundice, irregular menses, sciatica, scoliosis, general low back pain, lumbar spine strain, pain behind knee and back of the leg, cramping in calves, ankle sprain, ankle edema, Achilles tendonitis, pain along meridian path.

Kidney Meridian

The kidneys filter the blood and remove wastes which are excreted in the urine which continues its passage through the urinary system to the bladder.

The Kidney Meridian begins at the yongquan points on the sole of the foot. It continues up circling the inner ankle bone as it moves up the inner leg, continuing straight upwards to the side of the mid-line of the body, ending just below the clavicle.

Diseases and disorders associated with the Kidney Meridian are: Kidney problems, low back pain, slipped spinal discs L1-5, sacrum and coccyx pain, osteomyelitis, osteoporosis, fullness and pain in lower abdomen, abdominal distention, shortness of breath, panic attacks, heart failure, parathyroid dysfunctions, cough, fullness in chest, phlegm, external genital pain, prostate and uterine dysfunctions, nocturnal emissions, sexual dysfunction, pink urine, painful urination, constipation, vomiting, diarrhea, dorsal knee pain, ankle sprain, ankle edema, medial calf pain, burning sensation or pain on the sole of the foot, pain along meridian path.

Pericardium Meridian

The pericardium is a fibrous sac which surrounds the entire surface of the heart. Its inner layer consists of two membranes separated by fluid which helps to prevent friction as the heart beats. Its purpose is to shield and protect the heart.

The Pericardium Meridian begins at a point one inch from the outside of the nipple, goes up the shoulder, descends down the inner arm to the middle of the inner wrist, and ends at the tip of the middle finger.

Diseases and disorders associated with the Pericardium Meridian are: Cardiac pain, suffocating sensation in the chest, poor circulation, angina pectoris, palpitation, nausea, vomiting, dizziness, elbow and arm pain, painful, swollen arm pits, hot, sweaty palms, wrist pain, pain or stiffness in the middle finger, tremor of hand and arm, chest pain, stomach ache, pain in the gluteus maximus, or adductor muscles, pain along meridian path.

Sanjiao Meridian (Triple Warmer)

According to ancient Chinese physicians the Sanjiao (Triple Warmer) has a name but is without physical shape. The Sanjiao refers to three areas in the torso at the chest, between the diaphragm and the belly button, and the lower portion of the torso responsible for respiratory, digestive, and urogenital functions. The Sanjiao is a major source of the body's energy supply.

The Sanjiao Meridian starts at the tip of the ring finger and runs up the forearm, across the elbow to the back of the shoulder, up the side of the neck to the bottom of the ear, wraps around the ear and ends at the temple.

Diseases and disorders associated with the Triple Warmer Meridian are: Deafness, tinnitus, ear problems, sore throat, abdominal distension, facial nerve disorders, swelling of cheek and facial muscles, blurred vision, migraine, heart disorders, hypothalamus, pineal and pituitary disorders, hot flashes, cold chills, urinary incontinence, neck and shoulder pain, elbow pain, wrist pain, pain or stiffness in the ring finger, headache, toothache, irritability, pain along meridian path.

Gall Bladder Meridian

Lying right under the liver, the gall bladder is responsible for storing and secreting bile produced by the liver. The bile is sent down the intestine where it aids the digestive process.

The Gall Bladder Meridian begins at the outside corner of the eye, circles back up to the side of the forehead. From here it runs down the back of the head to the back of the shoulder, ascending up over the shoulder where it begins to flow down past the clavicle to a point underneath the armpit. At this point it flows down the rib cage to the side of the waist, to the pelvic crease. Finally, it flows down towards the side of the buttock where it continues down the outer leg to the outer portion of the ankle bone, ending at the tip of the fourth toe.

Diseases and disorders associated with the Gall Bladder Meridian are: Gall Bladder problems, tinnitus, blurred vision, vertigo, pain and stiffness in the neck, shoulder and upper back pain, headache, migraine, pain in lumbar region and thigh, swelling and pain in the knee, jaundice, vomiting, irregular menstruation, abdominal pain, weakness and numbness in the lower extremities, sleeping disorders, pain along meridian path.

Liver Meridian

The liver is responsible for performing vital chemical functions which includes processing of nutrients from the intestines; synthesizing proteins, sugars and fats; neutralizing poisons, and the conversion of waste to urea.

The Liver Meridian begins at the outside base of the big toe nail and ascends down the inside of the leg just above the pelvic crease. From here it then descends down to the groin area then re-ascends up the midline of the body about an inch below the naval. At this point it flows in a slight arc upwards from the waist to the ribcage at a point just below the sixth rib at the nipple.

Diseases and disorders associated with the Liver Meridian are: Liver problems, jaundice, hepatitis, Alzheimer's disease, memory loss, depression, lower abdominal pain, painful urination, external genital pain, lumbago, vomiting, diarrhea, indigestion, acid regurgitation, esophagus disorders, heart burn, thyroid disorders, bad breath, pituitary and hypothalamus dysfunctions, hernia, sexual disorders and dysfunctions, urination problems, lower abdominal pain, pain in medial aspect of knee and thigh, pain in the lower abdomen, lower abdominal distention, pain along meridian path.

The Ren Mai and Du Mai Meridians

Of all the meridians in the body the Ren Mai (Conceptual) Meridian and the Du Mai (Governing) Meridian are energetically most important. The other meridians in the body are viewed as streams or lakes, while the Ren Mai and Du Mai Meridians are considered to be seas.

Ren Mai Meridian (Conceptual)

The Ren Mai is a Yin vessel and is responsible for controlling all other Yin Zang meridians and organs. The Yin Zang meridians/organs are the heart, spleen, liver, lungs and kidneys.

The Ren Mai (Conceptual) Meridian starts just under the center of the lower lip and descends down the center of the body line into the huiyin a point just in front of the anus.

Diseases and disorders of the Ren Mai Meridian are: Lower abdominal pain, urinary frequency, urinary retention, irregular menstruation, morbid leukorrhea, uterine bleeding, indigestion, diarrhea, constipation, nausea, vomiting, hiccup, prolapse of rectum, hernia, distention and fullness in chest and costal region, chest pain, cough, breathing difficulties, swollen gums, toothache, and facial puffiness.

Du Mai Meridian (Governing)

The Du Mai is a Yang vessel and is responsible for governing all other Yang Fu meridians and organs. The Yang Fu meridians/organs are the gallbladder, stomach, small intestine, large intestine, bladder, colon, and Sanjiao (Triple Warmer).

The Du Mai Meridian begins at the chang qiang point just to the rear of the anus (at the coccyx), ascending up the midline of the spine to the top of the head, then down the center of the face ending at the middle of the upper lip.

Diseases and disorders of the Du Mai Meridian are: Pain and stiffness in the neck, back pain, lumbago, low back pain and stiffness, irregular menstruation, prolapse of rectum, prolapse of vagina, indigestion, leukorrhea, spinal problems, mental disorders, fever, headaches, vertigo, tinnitus, lip twitching, pain and swelling of gums.

Enhancing and Cleansing the Meridians

Meridians transport nutrient energy throughout the body, remove waste products from all body cells and coordinate all physiological and psychological functions. When a meridian becomes clogged or congested the flow of vital energy becomes stagnant causing illness to occur.

Cleansing, enhancing, and balancing the meridians are procedures that the JQS practitioner performs at each healing facilitation. By using certain techniques along the path of the meridian, and by manipulating the Xue points specific to the meridian being worked on, the JQS practitioner can clear and re-connect the flow of the energy pathways of the meridian vessels.

The technique of enhancing and cleansing energy in Traditional Chinese Medicine can be broken down into four components: empty, solid, enhance, and cleanse. When an illness is empty it refers to a condition that is weakening the body, and where the illness is not obvious. When working with an empty illness the basic principle is to enhance the client's vital energy. When an illness is solid it means that the nature of the illness is obvious and the basic principle would be to cleanse the client's vital energy. Quite simply, if and illness is empty you would enhance the vital energy, and if it is solid you would cleanse it.

Don't fret if the above seems a bit confusing to you at first. Most often both enhancing and cleansing is required. This is called the "even" principle and is the technique the JQS facilitator will use almost 90% of the time.

Early in my training as a JQS facilitator I became quite frustrated on how to know if a meridian needed enhancing or cleansing. I expressed my frustration to Xian Rinposhe and was told that all-in-all it really didn't matter. What was important was for me as the facilitator, to maintain the intention of wholeness in my patient's body. He went on to explain that on an innate level my patient's body knew what it needed to do to re-establish its natural state of wholeness, regardless of my approach when working with a particular meridian.

While observing my teacher working with patient's I noted that when he used a particular technique that went with the flow of a meridian that it had an enhancing effect. If he used a particular technique that went the opposite direction of the meridian flow, the effect was cleansing. More often than not, I observed Xian Rinposhe doing both on a meridian – going first opposite the meridian flow, and the going with the meridian flow. This is known as the "even principle" and is the preferred technique used by most JQS facilitators.

"Diagnosing" A Meridian

As a JQS practitioner, at this step of your healing facilitation you would have already gleaned clues as to what's going on inside your client by your scans of the aura, chakra's and your perceptive assessment of the organs in the body. The information collected from these scans is sufficient for you to determine which meridian(s) to work on. This being the case, the JQS practitioner does not really "diagnose" a particular meridian. The meridian is chosen based on what the facilitator has learned from his or her energy scans, and based on the client's symptoms and complaints.

For example, during a scan of your client's auric body you perceive coolness in the mid-to-low back. During your scan of the chakra you notice that the naval chakra appears to have a few shadowy spots in it. Your perceptive assessment confirms this. You may say to your client at this point, "I noted coolness in your low back. My scan of the naval chakra shows me an energetic disturbance too. Do you have pain in your low back?"

For the purpose of this example, your client answers with a "yes" and then tells you that he experiences a burning sensation while urinating. You would refer to the Meridian Symptoms/Deficiencies Chart (located in the Appendix) and determine the meridian's which would cause low back pain, and painful urination. Based on the chart you would have three meridians that match low back pain, and painful urination; the bladder, kidney, and liver meridians.

Of course, most of your clients will come to you with symptoms that they will share with you prior to beginning the healing facilitation. This provides you with immediate clues as to the direction of your three energy scans. This is helpful most of the time, however, my teacher always advocated energetically scanning your client first, and then ask them the purpose of their visit, as well as any additional questions concerning what you found during your scans. His reasoning was that he felt that sometimes a facilitator can miss indications of subtle energy deficiencies when he or she "thinks" they already know what's going on inside the body.

The most important thing when working with the meridians and the Xue points is to "reach the Qi". Imagine that you are reaching inside the client's body, through the clothes, skin, and body tissues, and touching the Qi flow.

If for some reason you cannot determine what meridian(s) to work with use the Du, Ren, and Sanjiao (Triple Warmer) Meridians. The Du and Ren Meridian affect every meridian and organ in the body, and the Sanjiao Meridian is a major source of the body's energy supply.

Exercise Fourteen. Cleansing and Enhancing Meridian Flow.

This exercise will teach you the even principle. The term "work" a meridian means the process of enhancing and cleansing a specific meridian. To do this the facilitator would sending healing Qi into the meridian via his or her finger by using the finger to draw along the meridian – first in the opposite direction of the meridian flow, and then in the regularly assigned direction with the meridian flow.

You can either touch the body as you lightly draw along the meridian path, or you can keep your finger about one inch above the skin. It's a matter of preference.

Preparation: Your client should be sitting on a stool or lying on the floor or a massage table. They should remain fully clothed. Feel free to consult the meridian charts in this book as you begin to learn the correct flow of each meridian. For the following exercise will be working with the Ren and Du Meridians since they have specific protocols that need to be addressed which are not a factor with the other meridians. The basic technique for the other meridians would be exactly the same and can be easily inferred.

1) Perform one to two minutes of full body Qi breathing. Remember: Spine straight, weight down, bellybutton pointed up, awareness on the dantian, tongue pressed against the upper palate!
2) When working with the Du and Ren Meridians always begin with the Du Meridian first without exception. If you are using a massage table the client would need to lay face down on their stomach. Using the index finger of your dominant hand (the hand you write with) start at the ending point of the Du Meridian which is at the center of the upper lip. Inhale, slowly, and smoothly, as you use your index finger to draw opposite the meridian path, over the middle of the head, down the centerline of the spine and stopping at a point just between the genitals and the anus. I scared you didn't I? You will *al-*

ways respect your client's modesty in a healing facilitation and will *never* actually touch your client's genitals or near the anus. At the starting point and ending point of the Du and Ren Meridians you would instruct your client to squeeze his or perineum once. The slow inhale, and the movement of the index finger over the meridian path are performed in one smooth, coordinated movement. As you draw your finger over the meridian visualize white healing Qi coming from your finger lighting up the meridian. Imagine that your finger is reaching inside the body into your client's Qi current. Silently affirm the word "cleansing" as you draw along the meridian. Exhale and relax.

3) Repeat steps one and two again. This means that you would have drawn the reverse flow of the meridian two more times.
4) Shake off your hands. Perform one to two minutes of Qi breathing.
5) Have your client squeeze his or her perineum. Starting at the beginning of the Du Meridian, inhale and slowly exhale silently affirming "strengthening". As you do this visualize white Qi energy lighting up the meridian path as you move your finger along the line of the meridian. The slow exhale and the movement of the index finger are performed in one smooth, deliberate motion. Relax your breathing.
6) Repeat step number five two more times making a total of three repetitions.
7) Shake off your hands and perform steps one through six on the Ren Meridian.

Note: The Du and Ren Meridians are the only meridians in which the client will need to squeeze the perineum. The squeezing motion stimulates the huiyin and chang qiang points which assisting the practitioner with stimulation of both of these hands off points.

The Xue Energy Points

After cleansing and enhancing the meridian flow the JQS practitioner will focus attention on the Xue energy points along the meridian. In Romanized Chinese Xue means vital points. Xue points are points on the skin where access to the vital flow of the energy of a meridian can be reached. The Xue points are where vital energy accumulates. It is essentially a magnified energy point. By stimulating this energy point with our finger we can affect the energy flow along the meridian we are working on. This allows for improved function and balance in meridians where deficiencies have manifested.

As indicated in a previous portion of this chapter, we have listed only the most important Xue points of each respective meridian. For a more detailed description of the Xue points and their function we recommend that you refer to a book on the subject of acupuncture.

Working with the Xue energy points compromises four basic techniques: pinching (nie), pressing (an), vibrating (zhen), and dotting (dian).

Pinching: The pinching technique is used to break up stagnant energy and clear blockages. With this technique you use the thumbs and index finger to raise a small amount of skin above the Xue point and then release it. It is not a conventional pinch were one feels pain.

Pressing: The pressing technique activates the energy flow throughout a meridian and cleanses its path. To perform this technique you would press the tip of your index finger (with light pressure) into a Xue point and hold it for about three seconds while sending healing Qi into the vital point.

Vibrating: The vibrating technique disseminates vital energy into the meridian. To perform this technique you would lightly press the tip of your index finger into a Xue point and quickly move your finger back and forth without lifting it from the energy point. You would continue the vibrating motion for three seconds while sending healing Qi into the vital point.

Dotting: This technique excites energy and blood flow, breaks up blockages and enhances and cleanses energy. It can be used with a Xue point and along the path of the meridian. To perform this technique you would lightly dot or tap the tip of your index finger for about three seconds on a Xue point while sending healing Qi, or dot gently along the path of the meridian while sending healing Qi into the meridian.

Tips for Working with the Xue Points:

1. Always perform one to two minutes of full body Qi breathing before you begin.
2. When working with the Xue points always go with the flow of the meridian (utilizing your choice of the four techniques) on the order the Xue points occur on the meridian path.
3. Apply light pressure on the Xue points. Make sure your fingernails are neatly trimmed.
4. Imagine your finger is reaching inside the meridian and touching the Qi current. Visualize the healing Qi being sent into the Xue point.
5. Do not perform more than three repetitions of three seconds on each Xue point.
6. Before going on to the Xue points on another meridian shake off your hands, and perform another one to two minutes of Qi breathing before you begin.

Summary of Chapter:

- The meridian system is a network of subtle energy flows inside the body.
- The flow of a meridian can be accessed and directed by the use of subtle energy, and by the manipulation of the Xue vital energy points along the meridian.
- The meridian system is classified into two main groups – primary and secondary.

- There are twelve primary meridians each of which is named for their specific relationship to the organ they represent, and how the organ processes energy.
- The Ren Mai (Conceptual), and the Du Mai (Governing) Meridians are energetically two of the most important meridians in the body.
- When a meridian becomes clogged or congested the flow of vital energy in the body stagnates causing illness to occur.
- Cleansing, enhancing, and balancing the meridians in the body restores the flow of vital Qi energy in the body.
- Xue points are vital energy points which can be accessed on the skin. Stimulating these vital points with subtle energy and a finger affects the energy flow along the meridian being worked on. This improves and strengthens the meridian being accessed.
- The four basic techniques used with Xue points are: pinching, pressing, vibrating, and dotting.

CHAPTER NINE

THE DIRECT QI HEALING TECHNIQUE

The Direct Qi Healing technique can be defined simply by its name. Healing Qi is sent directly where the client is feeling discomfort. To find this point the facilitator would ask the client "Show me where it hurts" (or where it's tight, where there is pressure, etc.). The facilitator would then go directly to the point of discomfort and draw and send healing Qi into the area either through direct touch, or with the hand(s) an inch or so above the area.

The Qi healing breath (full body Qi breathing) is used continuously during this technique. The continuous Qi breathing is the primary difference between the other techniques you have learned thus far in which you performed full body Qi breathing for one to two minutes at a time. The purpose of the full body Qi breathing for shorter bursts of time is to charge the dantian, which acts as a Qi reservoir. This reservoir fills with healing Qi energy to use with scanning, brushing, and cleansing the physical and energy bodies. During the direct healing Qi technique the facilitator's purpose is to raise their vibratory rate in order to cause the client to match that energy (resonance) thereby allowing a healing response to occur (entrainment). We have already discussed the process of vibration, resonance, and rhythm entrainment in previous chapters.

During the direct qi healing process the client may feel tightness, pain, discomfort, etc., move to another part of the body. I always instruct my clients during this process to inform me of any sensations he or she is experiencing. If the client tells me that the discomfort has moved or that they now feel a sensation in another area of the body, I go to the new area and continue with the Qi healing breath throughout the entire process. I would continue to draw and send healing Qi until my Higher Knowing tells me to stop, or when the client tells me that the discomfort has disappeared.

At times, during the direct Qi healing process your client may tell you that he or she feels heat coming from your hands. Even if the facilitator's hands do physically heat up, this is not to be misconstrued as anything but the practitioner's efficient blood circulation. More often than not, the heat the client feels is the body part or organ responding to the healing Qi being offered, and is a normal sensation during a healing facilitation.

Although JQS is a painless healing modality, there are times during a healing facilitation that your client may feel intense pain in a body part or organ. This sensation rarely lasts over five minutes and then dissipates. This sensation is normal and is what is termed in many energy healing modalities as a healing crisis. A healing crisis occurs as the body part or organs rapidly absorbs the healing energy and then quickly begins to entrain to the energy. A good way to explain this would be using the example of an open scrape wound which has been dowsed with hydrogen peroxide. The wound area would begin to bubble up and sting as it carried away germs and any dirt particles. After the area has been completely cleansed by the peroxide the burning sensation stops.

Should your client inform you of any pain or discomfort that is becoming more intense instruct them to breathe into the area they are feeling the discomfort. To illustrate, your client may tell you that she is beginning to feel sharp pains in her low back. Have her imagine that the area in the low back is sucking air into that area as she inhales, and then pushing the air out as she exhales. Stay on that area and continue to draw and send healing Qi until the client informs you that the pain has subsided. It's o.k. if your client's pain has lightened and has not resolved completely. The client's body will continue to entrain to the healing Qi for up to thirty six hours. For chronic conditions the client may need to return to additional sessions in order to loosen locked Qi. Locked Qi is dense energy that has locked in an area of the body over an extended length of time.

Your client is a valuable link during the direct Qi healing technique. Before you begin drawing and sending healing Qi, provide your client with a quick scenario of the sensations they may experience during the session and ask them to inform you of any sensations they may feel during the healing session.

Exercise Fifteen. The Direct Qi Healing Technique.

Note: Please pay special attention to your oral hygiene before administering this technique on your client. Avoid spicy foods and foods filled with garlic and/or onions before your session. Mouthwash, mints, brushing your teeth and tongue, are all very helpful. Also, please turn your head away from your client when exhaling. Your client will appreciate your respect and courtesy with proper oral hygiene, and for not exhaling right into his face, hair, neck, or where ever else you are creating a mini-wind storm with your exhalations.

Preparation: Your client may sit, stand, or lay down. Ask your client before you begin to show you where he or she may be experiencing discomfort. Sometimes there may be multiple areas. If this is the case ask your client to distinguish which body part has the greatest overall discomfort and work on that area first. Do not neglect any areas which you sensed need attention during your perceptive assessment.

1) Clap you hands together a couple of times and briskly rub them together to help activate your hand chakra. Make sure your body posture is comfortable (spine straight, belly-button up, weight sunk low).
2) Place your hands either directly over or directly touching the body part or organ indicated by the client, or by the perceptive assessment. Begin the Qi healing breath and continue to draw and send healing Qi into that specific area.
3) Check in with your client from time to time to see how they are doing. Don't get discouraged if your client indicates that they do not feel anything. Some people are more

tuned into their body than others are. If the client tells you that the pain or sensation moves to another part of the body, follow it continuing the Qi healing breath. Sometimes the facilitator will get and intuitive impression to move their hands elsewhere on the body. Follow these impressions.

4) The direct healing Qi session will end when either: you have an inner knowing that it is finished, the discomfort has disappeared, or the time allotted for the session has terminated.
5) Shake off your hands and sweep the energy off your hands and forearms.

Case History:

Gina N., Nurse Practitioner, Los Angeles, California – "The direct Qi healing technique is a quick and effective healing routine all on its own. My boyfriend Jeff and I had gone to dinner at a well known restraint chain. Jeff ate Chicken Picatta, and I chose Egg Plant Parmesan. A few hours later Jeff began to complain of severe gastric discomfort along with debilitating cramps. Jeff lay in fetal position no wanting to move. I quickly checked Jeff's vitals to make sure that he wasn't having a heart attack. I then scanned his stomach and gastro-intestinal area and "felt" sticky energy and "saw" what looked like bubbling lava running through his stomach and large intestine.

"I began to immediately draw and send healing Qi into Jeff's abdomen and upper and lower intestinal area intending to lessen the pain a bit before taking him to the ER. Jeff told me he experienced what he felt was extreme cold coming out of my hands. I continued my Qi healing breath for about 15 minutes moving my hands at random. At this point Jeff told me that the cramps had lessened. The pain in his abdomen, although still there lightened. I continued to draw and send healing Qi for another 10 minutes at which point Jeff's entire body began to heat up and he began to perspire profusely. Jeff who was now lying on his back with his eyes closed suddenly snapped them open and exclaimed, "The pain is gone!" I finished the session by sending healing Qi into the soles of Jeff's feet as I watched him as he fall into a deep sleep.

"I contacted the restaurant the following morning and found that 3 other patrons that night suffered from a severe bought of food poisoning. Jeff was the only patron who had not been hospitalized.

"Having attended a JQS workshop only on week prior to this incident I was thoroughly impressed with how effective the direct Qi healing technique is."

Of course as a JQS practitioner it is prudent to remember that you are not a medical doctor. Use your best judgment when facing an emergency medical situation.

Basic Hand Positions and Movements

During a direct Qi healing facilitation there are a variety of therapeutic hand positions the practitioner may choose from to cleanse, direct, and manipulate energy. Some of these hand positions you have learned in previous chapters.

The Flat Palm – The flat palm is one of the most commonly used hand positions a JQS practitioner uses during a healing facilitation. The practitioner sends healing Qi into an area on the body through the flat palm of the hand. The flat palm technique sends a broad beam of healing Qi into the area being worked on.

Palm Press - During a healing facilitation the JQS practitioner may lightly put one hand on the top of the body part being worked on and the other hand directly behind the area being worked on. Essentially the practitioner's hands are gently surrounding the area of the body part between the palms of the hands. This is known as the palm press technique. The palm press technique is another commonly used hand position that sends a concentrated broad beam of healing Qi into the area being worked on.

The Laser Finger – The laser finger directs healing Qi into a small concentrated area. To perform this technique the healing facilitator sends healing Qi through the tip of the index finger into the area being worked on.

The Chicken Beak - The thumb, index finger, and middle finger press together to form this hand position. In some Chinese martial art styles this finger position was used to "peck" or strike at the vital points of an opponent which helps to clarify its name. In JQS healing Qi is sent through the thumb and two fingers creating a slightly bigger energy field than that of the laser finger.

Scooping - This technique was explained in Exercise Eleven, How to Cleanse and Balance the Chakra. The hand is cupped and is used to remove thick, dense, knotted areas of stagnant energy in a particular area of the body. Always scoop the energy out counter-clockwise (from your viewpoint as if you were looking at a clock) and brush your hands off after a couple of passes.

Paint Brush - With this technique you use the fingers as if they were the bristles of a paint brush moving them smoothly in an up and down, or side to side manner. This technique is similar to auric brushing except that in auric brushing the hands only sweep downwards. The paint brush technique is used to smooth out the energy over and area causing your client discomfort to reduce pain.

Circling - Circling is done with either the flat of the palm or for a smaller area, a finger. Clockwise circling (from your viewpoint as if you were looking at a clock) tonifies an area being treated. Tonifying adds energy, heat, and stimulation to an area being treated. You would use clockwise circling in areas where you sensed a feeling of coolness or cold.

Counter clockwise circling takes away excess energy, heat, and inflammation. Counter clockwise circling is known as sedating. You would use this technique in areas of infection, and for inflammation and swelling in muscles or joints.

Simplified, clockwise circling (tonifying) adds energy, and counter clockwise circling (sedating) takes out excess energy.

Pulsing – Pulsing is done with either the relaxed flat of the palm, or with the finger for a smaller area. The relaxed flat of the palm or a finger gently pulses over areas where stagnant Qi energy is sensed. This technique stimulates Qi without adding excess heat.

Always brush your forearms and hands off after use of hand positions in which you energetically reach in to scoop out energy, or in those win which you tonify or sedate energy. Doing so will discharge dirty Qi buildup that may have attached to your hands and forearms.

Summary of Chapter:

- The direct healing Qi technique is used to send healing Qi directly into the area of discomfort.
- The Qi healing breath (full body Qi breathing) is performed continuously when drawing and sending healing Qi.
- Have your client inform you of any sensations he or she is experiencing. If the discomfort seems to move to another area of the body, follow it.
- Sometimes the pain or discomfort in an area may seem to increase in intensity. This is what is called a healing crisis. Continue working on the area until the discomfort decreases or goes away.
- The direct Qi healing facilitation ends when either you have an inner knowing that it is finished, the clients discomfort disappears, or when the time allotted for that part of the session has expired.
- There are eight therapeutic hand positions a facilitator may choose from during a direct Qi healing facilitation. The hand positions are used to cleanse, direct, and manipulate energy.
- Always brush off your hands and forearms after use of hand positions in which you energetically reach in to scoop out energy, or in those in which you tonify or sedate energy. This discharges any dirty Qi which may have attached to your hands and forearms.

CHAPTER TEN

THE USE OF SOUND AND COLOR IN HEALING

History of Sound Healing

The use of sound to facilitate healing can be traced back as early as the Qin Dynasty (221-207 B.C.). In fact, sound healing has been used a stimulus to facilitate healing for thousands of years. From ancient Greece to the Tibetan monasteries, incantations, song, melody, and rhythm have been used by virtually every ancient civilization to cure diseases of the body, mind, and soul.

What Sound Healing Is and How It Works

Sound Healing is the therapeutic application of sound frequencies to the body with the intent of re-establishing health and harmonic balance.

The ears are said to be among one of our most important sense organs. The ears control the body's sense of balance and are the conductor of the entire nervous system. Through the medulla, the auditory nerve connects with all the muscles in the body. Your muscle tone, equilibrium, flexibility, and vision, are all affected by sound. Through the vagus nerve, the inner ear connects with the larynx, heart, lungs, stomach, liver, bladder, kidneys, small intestine and large intestine.

So how exactly does sound healing work? As with that of most energy healing arts, JQS included, how sound healing works is best explained by the scientific principles of resonance and entrainment. Every organ, bone and cell in the body has its own unique resonant frequency. Together they can be viewed as an orchestra playing one beautiful song. Each organ, bone, and cell represents its own unique frequency or orchestral sound. Where one instrument is out of tune, it affects the entire orchestra. This is true in the body as well. When one system or organ is out of "tune" the entire body is affected. The use of sound can be used to help the diseased organ back into harmonic resonance by causing the organ to entrain (match) the resonant vibration of the healing source. The principle of entrainment states that powerful rhythmic vibrations from one source will cause the less powerful vibrations from another source to lock into vibration with the first, more powerful source.

Tools of Sound Healing

There are many tools a sound healing practitioner may use in their healing session. Tuning forks, as well as Tibetan singing bowls in various frequencies have been used to help build up healing resonances in the diseased organ. Bells with different ring tones, drums in various sizes and tones, flutes, stringed instruments, etc., may also be used according to the sound healer's preference.

The primary tool used in JQS, and one of the most effective, is that of the human voice. Scientific studies have shown that making a specific sound frequency with the voice produces the same effect as that of tuning forks or other instruments. This process is known as "toning" and simply means humming, singing, or vibrating a certain tone frequency either aloud or sub vocally.

Exercise Sixteen. Toning Technique to Balance the Chakras.

This exercise is an extension to the instructions on how to balance the chakra, as found in Exercise Twelve of Chapter Six. The toning technique would be initiated at step four of the instructions. As you visualize the white healing Qi radiating from your hands you would add the component of sound to what you are doing – either vibrating the sound aloud, or sub-vocally. The healing tone you would be using will be dependant upon which chakra you are attempting to balance. For a list of the healing tones associated with the each chakra refer to Chapter Six.

The toning technique consists of inhaling through the nose and exhaling through the mouth as you emit the healing tone associated to each individual chakra. In essence, for the solar plexus chakra, as you visualize the white healing Qi flowing from your hands you would also then vibrate the sound of 'RAHHHmmm' on the exhale. For the naval chakra, as you visualized sending the white light, inhale, and then vibrate the sound of 'VAHHHmmm' on the exhale, and so forth.

Color and Healing

The use of color therapy for purposes of facilitating healing in the body originated from the ancient cultures of India, China, and Egypt. Color medicine, or chromotherapy, was developed into its current state by Dr. Dishna P. Ghadiali, a physician from India.

Charles Klotsche, author and holistic color healer, says the following about Dishna in his book *Color Medicine*: "Dishna had special understanding of color medicine. Not only did he recognize the necessity of attunement of the healing colors with the chakras, but he also realized that by using the visible spectrum only there could be no healing effects. Colors and other vibrations continually surround us, penetrating our bodies even though we cannot see or relate to them with our physical body or other senses."

Concerning how the use of color to affect healing works Klotsche explains, "This therapy isolates and accents various colors of the spectrum and their corresponding vibrations, applying them to ailing parts of the aura and the body to restore emotions as well as damaged cells, tissues, or restricted energy flows through . . . systematic methods . . . there is a unique color or energy vibration that either sedates or stimulates the stream of energy through a specific organ causing a biochemical reaction."

Although Chromotherapists use a special high spectrum light, the vibratory rates of visualized colors sent to specific areas of the body also quite effective. I have also had the opportunity to witness one of my teachers combining the use of color with energy medicine by charging a colored piece of cotton flannel with Qi healing energy and then applying it to a patient's wrist. I watched in amazement as the swelling in the joint began to subside within ten minutes of its application.

Healing Principles of Color

Of course, the list below is quite basic revealing mostly primary colors, but it's a great starting point to help gain a basic understanding of the use of color and healing. JQS emphasizes respecting the potency of the vibratory rates of the colors sent to a client by using a toned down version of the color and amplifying it deeper if necessary.

White: Purification, stabilizing, the all purpose color. Use this color when you are not sure which color to use. It is beneficial to all systems in the body.

Black: Grounding, protection. Black gets a bad rap. Black is actually a protective color. Avoid using too much of this color as it could bring on depression. This color is never used alone, but with a combination of colors.

Green: Balance, general healing, growth. Used for circulatory system, emotional conditions, and conditions related to the heart chakra. Do not use this color for cancerous or tumor like conditions since green is a color of growth.

Red: Stimulating, strengthening, warming. Used for circulatory system, sexuality, stimulating the over all energy of the metabolism, and for most blood conditions. Do not use red in cases of hypertension.

Blue: Cooling, calming, cleansing, restructuring. Used for respiratory, eyes, ears, nose, asthma, high blood pressure.

Yellow: Awakening, mental stimulation, used for most conditions related to the solar plexus chakra, especially the digestive system, stomach, intestines, adrenal function, and bladder.

Orange: Activating, constructing. Used for spleen, pancreas, stomach, food assimilation, eliminative system, and most conditions related to the naval chakra.

Indigo: Purification. Used for endocrine system, lymph system, immune system, blood purifier, conditions of the ears, nose, throat.

Lavender: Purification, cleansing. Used for skeletal system, nervous system, balancing of physical and spiritual energies.

Pink: Soothing, nurturing. Used for the immune system, thymus gland, skin conditions, inflammation, and helping to soothe emotional disturbances.

Gold: Restructuring, strengthening. Used for cardiac system, the entire immune system.

Exercise Seventeen. Sending Color During a Direct Qi Healing Facilitation.

This exercise would be carried out exactly as that of Exercise Fifteen of Chapter Nine except that the following component would be added to step number two:

As you draw healing Qi from the earth imagine it to be the appropriate healing color for the objective of your facilitation (i.e., white for stabilizing, blue for cooling, lavender for purification, etc.). As you send the healing Qi imagine flooding the area being treated with the chosen color.

Summary of Chapter:

- The use of sound to facilitate healing can be traced back as early as the Qin Dynasty (221-207 B.C.). Virtually every ancient civilization has used sound to cure diseases of the body, mind, and soul.
- Sound Healing is the therapeutic application of sound frequencies to the body with the intent of re-establishing health and harmonic balance.
- As with that of most energy healing arts, how sound healing works is best explained by the scientific principles of resonance and entrainment. Every organ, bone and cell in the body has its own unique resonant frequency.
- The primary sound tool used in JQS, and one of the most effective, is that of the human voice.
- Toning is the process in which one hums, sings, or vibrates a certain tone frequency either aloud or sub-vocally.

- All colors have a unique vibratory frequency that can either sedate or stimulate the stream of healing energy through a specific organ causing a bio chemical reaction to occur.
- When sending color to an organ or body part, start out with its pastel equivalent first and deepen the shade as needed. Never start out drawing and sending the highest frequency of the color shade.

PART THREE

The Treatment Session & Treatment Protocols

This section will teach the JQS facilitator how to put it all together by providing instructions for the Direct Qi Healing Technique, the use of color and sound in a healing facilitation, distance scanning and distance healing facilitations, a complete breakdown of the treatment session, along with a few final considerations for the JQS practitioner.

As an added bonus, instructions for a wellness treatment as well as treatment protocols for some common ailments and conditions are provided as a springboard for building up your treatment regimen.

CHAPTER ELEVEN

THE JING-QI-SHEN TREATMENT SESSION

In this chapter I have broken down the JQS treatment session into individual components and will explain each section in detail where needed. When facilitating a healing session it is important to remember that a JQS practitioner always works from the outside of the energy body inwards to the biological body.

Length of Session

I am often asked how long a healing facilitation takes. The length of the session generally depends upon the experience of the practitioner, and upon the condition of dissonant energy being manifested in the client's energetic and physical bodies. Sessions can last anywhere from 45 minutes up to an hour and a half. I find the following true in reference to time frames:

All Scans (auric, chakra, and perceptive assessment) – 10 to 15 minutes *combined.*
Chakra Clearing and Balancing - 10 to 15 minutes *combined.*
Auric Brushing - 5 to 10 minutes.
Meridian Work – 5 to 10 minutes.
Direct Qi Healing – 15 to 20 minutes plus.
Concluding – 5 minutes.

The above is certainly not set in stone. Sometimes you will need to spend more time on one or more of the session segments. Never try to rush a session. Follow your intuitive guidance on how long you need to spend on each client's particular needs.

As I indicated in previous sections of this manual, you can always scan the auric layer and chakra of your client *before* they arrive for their session. I like to do this from time to time, especially when my appointment book is full.

Exercise Eighteen. Distance Scanning.

Preparation: Find a quiet place where you won't be disturbed by pets, children, your spouse, or a telephone. It is best to sit on a chair or sofa while performing this exercise. Your feet should be flat on the floor. I am not that tall so to remedy dangling feet I move my body forward until my feet touch the floor. This allows my spine to remain straight. If you feel that you need back support, place some pillows behind you as a bolster.

You should always have a pad of paper with your client's name and birthday written on top of the page. Have two writing utensils handy making sure that they function properly. I have found by experience that pencil leads break, and pens run out of ink, so by preparing ahead of time you will not need to severe your intuitive focus by getting up and searching for another writing utensil.

1) Close your eyes. Take a few deep breaths. Relax your body progressively, starting first with both feet. Imagine feeling warmth and relaxation in both feet. Fell the warmth and relaxation moving up your ankles, calves, all the up to your hips, your torso, our hands and arms, your neck, and your scalp and facial muscles. DO NOT NEGLECT THIS STEP. This relaxation technique is important as it slows your brain wave pattern to that of alpha.
2) Perform one to two minutes of Qi breathing.
3) Mentally state your intention. In this case you would silently declare, "It is my intention to scan the aura (chakra, physical body) of [your client's name] who was born on [birth date]. Show me the front and back of the auric body. Thank you, it is done."
4) Begin to notice what you see in your minds eye and trust all of your first impressions. What you see isn't your imagination. Record everything you see, feel, or "know" to be true. For example, for the auric layer, record any spots, blobs, dark mists, etc. and note where on the auric layer you perceive them. Is there a dark mist near the back of the neck? Perhaps you intuitively see some small brown spots on the area around the liver.
5) Repeat steps 1-4 for the chakra and perceptive scans.

Tips on Distance Scanning

Auric Scan: Some students find it helpful to visualize a silhouette of their client inside a large egg as they perform distance scanning.

Chakra Scan: For distance scanning of chakra most students prefer to visualize their client's chakra as if they have been superimposed onto a photographers light box (similar to the fluorescent light boxes the medical profession uses to display ex-rays).

Perceptive Assessment: For full body distant scanning students are split between the two following techniques:

1. Visualize a clear blue silhouette of the client and as you scan from the top of the head to the feet imagine turning a light on inside of each of the body organs and bones being scanned.
2. Visualize a silhouette of the client and imagine yourself going inside the top of your client's head and lighting up each organ or bone as you intuitively view from inside their body as you scan downward.

Some students like to draw what they see in the auric and chakra scans. This is a matter of preference. Drawing what you see is a fun exercise and can help the beginning facilitator to visually record their impressions.

Once you have performed your distance scans and have taken the time to evaluate your perceptions you cam double check your findings quickly when you client arrives for the healing facilitation. Quickly scan the auric body and chakra system paying extra attention to the areas you noted energy disturbances. If, for example, one of the distance scans revealed dark energy around a client's lower intestine, the facilitator will pay closer attention to this area to obtain additional information with a quick scan when the client is physically present for the session.

The JQS Healing Session

Typically a JQS healing facilitation follows the following sequence:

1. Request Divine assistance - God, Buddha, Jesus, Angeles, Spiritual Guides, etc.
2. Ground and connect client.
3. Perform the three scans (auric layer, major chakra, and perceptive assessment).
4. Formulate healing plan of action.
    a) Clear auric layer.
    b) Clear and balance chakra.
    c) Clear appropriate meridian(s).
5. Perform direct Qi healing technique.
6. Seal physical and auric layers.
7. Decord from client.
8. Thank Spiritual assistance.

We will explain each of these segments in detail below. But first, let's discuss pre-session preparation.

Preparation Before the Session

Make sure that the healing environment is as free from distractions as possible. Soothing music, small water features, incense, candles, and similar effects help to set a tranquil environment, but are optional. I enjoy making the healing environment as comfortable as possible for myself as well as the client.

The JQS practitioner should be a clean, empty, energy conduit. As such, the facilitator should take a few minutes before the appointment to cleanse and balance his or her auric layers and chakra. Refer the section on energy hygiene in Chapter Twelve.

Have a box of facial tissues nearby. Releasing energy from a client's body ma bring up intense feelings, including tears. If this occurs softly instruct the client to allow the emotions to emerge and remind them that they are in a safe environment to do so. Continue with the healing facilitation and allow the client their emotional state.

Finally, feel free to have this manual nearby so that you can consult it for the proper course of meridian pathways, Xue points, and treatment formulation should the need arise.

When the client arrives for his or her appointment take a few minutes to explain what things they can expect during a JQS facilitation. This simple courtesy helps to ease any apprehensions the client may have and can help them to relax during the session. This is also the time to have the client give you a general idea of why they are there for the session. Write this information down and make notes of any physical symptoms.

1. **Requesting Divine Assistance:** Prayer is a wonderful and effective way to center yourself and your client spiritually and is an incredible way to increase your vibratory rate. Most facilitators ask assistance from the Supreme Deity of their faith, and to the angels and spiritual guides associated with that Supreme Deity. However, your spiritual tradition is not as important as is your willingness to surrender in love to the flow and distribution of healing energy. Your request for Divine assistance is a silent or verbal statement.

My teacher, Xian Rinposhe verbally recites the Medicine Buddha Prayer in his native tongue, and asks the Medicine Buddha, and Shakimuni Buddha to be present during the healing facilitation, and to allow him to clearly channel healing energy to his client.

I silently call upon Divine Source, Jesus, the Arch Angel Raphael, my Healing Guides, Kuan Yin, and the Medicine Buddha. My prayer is as follows: "Holy One, Mother, Father, Divine Source, I allow myself to be a clear conduit of healing energy and love during this healing facilitation. Surround me and fill me with the healing power of Jesus, the Arch Angel Raphael, the Medicine Buddha, Kuan Yin, and my Healing Guides for the benefit all concerned. Thank you, it is done, it is done, it is done."

My friend Timothy, a Native American Shaman, sincerely asks, "Great Spirit, may I see with your eyes, may I touch with your hands, and may I love with your Heart so that health and wholeness may be restored."

2. **Ground and Connect Client:** Grounding and connecting the client is a technique in JQS known as "connecting heaven to earth". This technique grounds and centers the client's physical and spiritual energies. To perform the technique place your hands and inch or two above the top of your client's head. Close your eyes and visualize a brilliant white beam of lightening coming down from heaven, piercing through your client's head (the baihui point) down the center of his or her body, and deep into the earth.

As a matter of etiquette do not directly touch the top of your client's head. In many Asian cultures and spiritual disciplines touching the top of someone's head would be considered quite rude and very disrespectful. Please respect your client's crown chakra.

3. **Scan Auric Layer, Major Chakra, and perform Perceptive Assessment.** Make mental notes of areas that are either hot, cold, lumpy, uneven, heavy, sticky, and areas that you can in-

tuitively see dark mists, blotches, spots, etc. Pay attention to any emotions (fear, sadness, anger, etc.) or symbolic pictures that may present themselves during your scans.

If you wish to physically jot down notes of your impressions during your scans, do so after each scan you perform so that you will not forget anything.

4. **Formulate Healing Plan of Action:** In the appendix of this course manual we have provided the facilitator with treatment protocols for a variety of common ailments. You can use these treatment regimens during your healing facilitation, or you can develop your own by reviewing the information provided on the characteristics of the chakra, the meridian functions, and the healing color and sound chapter. To formulate your own treatment plan you would look up the energy deficiencies being manifested and ascertain which chakra, meridians, and if you wish to incorporate them into your healing facilitation – color and sound, correlates with your client's needs.

Once you have an idea of where the energy and/or physical disturbances in the body are work from outside inwards by doing the following:

A. Brush auric layer. Brush each section of the front of the body six times per section. Do the same for the back of the body.
B. Cleanse and Balance Chakra.
C. Clear appropriate meridian(s).

After the clearing and balancing is completed your chosen healing action plan would now be initiated. Don't forget your perfect posture, belly-button "up", weight sunk low, attention on dantian.

5. **Perform Direct Qi Healing Technique:** [Note: For a General Wellness treatment skip this step and go directly to step six.] Go directly to the areas where you noted energetic disturbances from you perceptive assessment, and then to any parts of the client's body where physical pain or discomfort is manifesting. If your client's low back hurts, you would perform the direct Qi healing technique to the low back. If the client's left elbow is hurting, then you would place your hands there. You get the idea.

When drawing and sending energy don't forget to send the appropriate healing color into the area you are concentrating on as well.

6. **Seal Physical and Auric Layers:** After the treatment session is complete have your client lie on his or her back on the massage table, mat, or the floor. Make sure they are comfortable. I roll up both towels and use them as bolsters placing one underneath the client's neck and one underneath the client's knees.

To seal the physical and auric layers, sit or stand at your client's feet. Place one palms of each of your hands over the soles of the client's feet. Draw and send healing Qi into both feet.

In your minds eye see brilliant white light travel through your client's body up to the top of their head. Once it reaches the head, visualize the energy expanding out from every part of your client's body until it extends out about four feet in circumference from your client's body. You can end the session at this point, or you can send color through your client's feet.

I like to send a rainbow of color through the client's feet. Sometimes I also ask the client to quickly think of a color and tell me what it is. I then, relying on their intuition, send that color.

7. **Decord From Client:** Sometimes during a healing facilitation an energetic connection with your client is formed in the area of the solar plexus. This is called energetic cording.

To decord yourself after each session swiftly sweep your hand down karate chop style down the front of your body (palm facing toward you) and then back up again. Perform this vigorous hand motion a couple of times.

8. **Thank Spiritual Helpers for Their Assistance.**

After the Session

When the session is complete the facilitator should sweep off excess energy from the hands and forearms and then rinse the hands with water. Both the facilitator and the client should drink six to eight ounces of water. This helps to ground the healing Qi. I like to buy individual bottles of water to present to my client after the session.

Always take some time to debrief with the client after the session, and inform the client that their body will continue to entrain to the Qi healing energy for up to 36 hours. If time permits, I encourage my clients to share with me things they may have experienced during the healing facilitation. Clients respond to healing Qi in various ways. The experiences and stories they share always fascinate me prompting me to record them in my personal journals.

Distance Healing Facilitations

A distance healing facilitation does not differ much from a session in which the client is physically present. In a distance healing facilitation, the practitioner visualizes the client in front of him or her as if the client is actually present for the session. If it helps, you may also use a doll or stuffed animal to represent your client. This practice has been around for centuries and many ancient indigenous cultures have used dolls, or poppets in their healing practices to represent their patient. In some native cultures the dolls were constructed with healing herbs and even included a piece of hair or some blood from the person the doll was being constructed for.

Modern Magickal traditions call this technique sympathetic magick. Whether you use a stuffed animal or other item to intuitively tune into your client, or just visualize your client before you, what is most important is your intention to facilitate health and wholeness to the intended client.

What if you don't know what the client looks like? If you don't know what the client looks like, which will be the case in many distance healing facilitations, just visualize them as a blue human silhouette, or as a white luminous being.

To perform a distance healing facilitation proceed with the distance scanning as presented in the paragraphs above. It is VERY IMPORTANT to make sure that you pay attention to step number one of the instructions. The necessity for relaxation is imperative for your intuition to operate at its peak.

When you have completed your scans you are ready to proceed to steps one through eight of the JQS healing facilitation, adjusting where necessary. You would continue with the facilitation *as if the client was actually in front of you.*

I perform all of my auric brushing, and chakra cleansing and balancing on my visualized client as if they were actually present in the room with me. For meridian clearing, direct Qi healing, and for sealing the physical and auric layers, I many times use my well loved, over sized stuffed Winnie-the Pooh. This is just what is comfortable for me. You can use what ever method works best for you. For the direct Qi healing, one of my students imagines that she shrinks her clients so that they fit in the palm of her hand. She then draws and sends energy to them in her cupped hands.

Summary of Chapter:

- The length of a JQS healing facilitation depends on the experience of the practitioner and the condition of the energy being manifested in the client's energetic and/or physical body.
- Distance scanning can help to cut down the length of a session if necessary.
- Before the healing session the facilitator should make sure that the environment is free from distraction, is as comfortable as possible, and should cleanse their energetic body.
- When the client arrives for the session the JQS practitioner should take a few minutes to explain to the client what he or she can expect during a JQS healing facilitation.
- Asking for Divine Assistance (prayer) spiritually centers the client and the healing facilitator, and increases their vibratory rate.
- The JQS session always begins working on the outside of the client's energetic body (auric layer) and works inward to the chakra, energy meridians, and to the physical body.

- After the session the facilitator and the client should drink six to eight ounces of water. If time permits, the facilitator should spend a few minutes to debrief with the client and allow them to share what things they experienced during the session.
- A distance healing facilitation does not differ much from a session in which the client is physically present. In a distance healing facilitation, the practitioner visualizes the client in front of him or her as if the client is actually present for the session.

CHAPTER TWELVE

CONSIDERATIONS FOR THE PRACTITIONER

The purpose of this chapter is to provide the JQS facilitator a solid foundation on which to build an energy healing practice. I believe that the following information is beneficial whether or not the facilitator intends to facilitate healings on a full-time or part-time basis, and regardless if the practitioner collects a fee for services, or prefers to facilitate without charge.

This chapter will discuss professional ethics of the energy practitioner, and of course the physical, energetic, and spiritual considerations for the healing facilitator.

Professional Ethics

First and foremost please remember that you are not a medical doctor. As such, use extreme caution when discussing your findings with a client. *Never* diagnose or prescribe unless you are licensed to do so.

When I discuss my energetic findings with a client I never tell my client "I see dark spots on your liver. This means you have cancer." Such a statement can throw a practitioner in jail for practicing medicine without a license.

A more responsible reply could be – "My scans indicate some disturbances in the flow of Qi energy in your solar plexus chakra, and around your liver and gallbladder area." In this particular instance the facilitator is just relaying to the client what they have perceived. If the client then asks, "Does this mean that I have X-Y-Z condition?" I would remind them that what I perceive is just stagnant Qi energy that needs to be cleared. If they persist I politely remind them that I am not a medical doctor.

A high percentage of client's who come for a JQS facilitation come with physical symptoms or energetic disturbances that have already manifested symptoms such as headache, fever, stomach ache, fatigue, etc. If you ever feel an inner intuitive nudge that the client needs to see a medical doctor politely note your concerns to your client. I had a client make an appointment for, as she termed it, "a minor skin rash". When she arrived for her appointment her skin rash was anything but minor. Some areas of her skin had even erupted with seeping scabs. I politely told her that I felt that she needed to see a medical doctor and that I was not equipped to handle her immediate medical situation. Even though I could have sent healing Qi throughout her body to help her skin and sores begin to heal themselves, my intuition told me otherwise.

While discussing professional ethics at a recent advanced JQS workshop Mandy, a fairly new JQS practitioner (and a Licensed Vocational Nurse) relayed the following story to our group. Her roommate's brother had presented himself for a healing facilitation with symptoms of weakness, stomach upset, and diarrhea. She took his temperature with a forehead thermometer and was surprised to find a temperature of 103°. When she told him about his high temperature he answered, "Oh, is it still that high?" Upon further questioning she found that he had a high temperature with the other symptoms for five days since his return from a fishing trip in Mexico. She also found out that he had been unable to keep fluids or food in his system. Mandy told her roommate of her brother's condition and told her that she believed he needed medical attention immediately, at which point he was taken to the nearest hospital ER. Consequently he was admitted immediately due to dehydration and a diagnosis of dysentery. The major point is to always use common sense when facilitating a JQS session.

During a healing facilitation the client's physical boundaries should also be respected. The client's session should take place fully clothed. The only things that need be removed are the client's watch, jewelry, eyeglasses, belt, and shoes and socks.

When a client calls to make an appointment I always suggest that they wear comfortable natural fiber clothes such as cotton or cotton blends. Natural fiber absorbs healing Qi quite readily while synthetic fibers do not.

Personal Hygiene

We briefly discussed the importance of personal hygiene in a previous chapter. Be considerate of your client by presenting yourself with clean hands and a clean body. Do not wear perfume or cologne. Some client's may be allergic or may find the scents offensive. Make sure that your teeth have been brushed and that your breath is fresh. It is also a good idea to avoid eating spicy food, onions or garlic, before scheduled appointments.

Energetic Hygiene

Special attention should be given to the continued maintenance of the JQS facilitator's energetic hygiene. The chakra and energetic body should be cleansed and balanced on a regular basis. The Qi healing breath should also be practiced on a daily basis whenever you have the opportunity. This helps to keep the practitioner's vibratory rate humming with optimal efficiency.

The practice of yoga and Qigong are also excellent vehicles for helping to maintain the JQS practitioner's energetic hygiene.

One's thoughts and emotions also have specific impact on the body's energetic hygiene. Special care of how you think and how you feel is mandatory for proper etheric hygiene. Pay close attention to the lyrics of the music you listen to, the things you read, and the subject content of television programs and motion pictures. Viewing, listening to, or reading about violence, killing, foul language, disrespectful comments about other people, etc. are energetic scabs. These scabs feed on the energetic, physical, and spiritual bodies and vibrate at low energy levels.

If an activity, a thought, or an emotion does not enhance greater cosmic consciousness with peace and love avoid it.

Spiritual Practice

A consistent spiritual practice is of great benefit to the JQS facilitator. Prayer, meditation, and quiet sitting keep the entire physical, spiritual, and energetic bodies balanced. Learn to respect and acknowledge your spiritual divinity, and learn to respect the spiritual divinity of another. We are all spiritual beings in a physical body having a human experience.

Continue to enrich yourself in your spiritual tradition with dedicated study, and allow others to do the same without criticism. Always remember that we all vibrate spiritually in the One Song (Universe) in love, which is the highest and purest vibration there is.

The Business of Healing

If you wish to facilitate healings for others as a business, check with your state, county, or city first regarding any possible regulations that may exist. Many states allow holistic and alternative health businesses without a professional license. JQS, Reiki, Pranic Healing, and Hands on Healing are not massages and there is little to no body contact involved. Most states have no regulations prohibiting their practice. Some states may require that the practitioner be a member of the clergy in order to perform healing services. If this is your city or states policy, and you are planning to attend seminary, then good for you. If not, there is an easier way. You can become ordained for free by the Universal Life Church by simply going on line at www.ulc.com and applying for ordination.

As with any business entity, keep yourself legal. Obtain a business license and keep your tax records in good order. There are many free resources and educational tutorials for new business start ups available online from the Small Business Administration, www.sba.gov.

Summary of Chapter:

- Never diagnose or prescribe. You are not a medical doctor.
- Respect your client's physical boundaries.
- Make sure your personal hygiene is impeccable. Bathe regularly and avoid colognes or perfumes if you are going to facilitate a healing.
- Have clean, fresh breath.
- Do not eat spicy food, onions or garlic before an appointment.
- Pay attention to your etheric hygiene. Your energetic body and your chakra should be cleansed and balanced on a regular basis.

- Be mindful of your thoughts, emotions, and activities.
- Have a consistent enriching spiritual practice.

Appendix A:

Jing-Qi-Shen Treatment Protocols

Below I have taken the liberty to list treatment protocols for 50 common ailments. These treatment protocols would be used in conjunction with the Jing-Qi-Shen Treatment Session, and be initiated beginning at step number six. Steps number one through five should be completed as instructed. However, it is imperative that step number five (brushing auric layer, cleansing and balancing chakras, clearing appropriate meridians) be thoroughly completed *before* initiating the desired treatment.

Key:

LU – Lung Meridian
LI – Large Intestine/Colon Meridian
ST – Stomach Meridian
SP – Spleen Meridian
HT – Heart Meridian
SI – Small Intestine Meridian
BL – Bladder Meridian
KI – Kidney Meridian
PC – Pericardium Meridian
SJ – Sanjiao Meridian
LR – Liver Meridian
GB – Gall Bladder Meridian
RN – Ren Mai Meridian
DU – Du Mai Meridian

C7 – Crown Chakra
C6 – Third Eye Chakra
C5 - Throat
C4 - Heart
C3 – Solar Plexus
C2 - Naval
C1 – Root

Anxiety – See Wellness Treatment

Arm Pain – For general muscular or joint pain in the arm, apply local brushing over area of discomfort, brushing downwards (towards the fingers). For wrist pain, work LU and LI meridians. For forearm pain, work LI and ST meridians. For elbow pain work LI, SI, SJ, meridians. For biceps pain, work LU and LI meridians. For triceps pain, work SP meridian. Place your dominant hand over C4 and draw and send white healing qi into the area as you move the palm of your hand in a clockwise motion (do this for one minute). If you sensed heat in the area affected or if there is inflammation, place the palm of your dominant hand over the area and move the palm in a counter clockwise motion (ten passes) with the intention of taking out excess qi energy. Perform paint brush hand technique over the area as you draw and send light green qi and then light blue qi. Sandwich affected body part between the palms and perform Direct Qi Healing continuing to draw and send light green and light blue qi into the area.

Back Ache (Sciatica, Lumbago, Spinal Conditions) – For general pain in the upper, middle and lower back and Sciatica, apply local brushing over entire spine from neck to coccyx. For pain in the upper back work BL, GB, DU meridians. For mid-back pain work BL, GB, DU meridians. For low back pain, lumbago and sciatica work BL, KI, LR, GB, and DU meridians. Place your dominant hand over C3 and draw and send white healing qi into the area as you move your hand in a clockwise motion (do this for one minute. Place your dominant hand over C1 (at the base of tailbone) and draw and send white healing qi into the area as you move the palm of your hand in a clockwise motion (do this for one minute). For sciatica and low back problems also place your dominant hand over C2 (dantian) and draw and send white healing qi into the area as you move the palm of your hand in a clockwise motion (do this for one minute). If you sensed heat in the area affected or if there is inflammation, place the palm of your hand over the area and move the palm of your dominant hand in a counter clockwise motion (ten passes) with the intention of taking out excess qi energy. Perform paint brush hand technique over the area as you draw and send light green qi and then light blue qi. Place your hands over the painful area and draw and send light green qi, and then light blue qi. Place your hands over both of the client's hips and draw and send light green qi, and then light blue qi into the hips.

Bells Palsy – Apply local area brushing to the front and back aspect of C3, C4, and the liver area. Work LI, ST, SI meridians. Place your hands over the front aspect of C3 and draw and send light green healing qi into the area as you imagine the healing qi spiraling into the area clockwise, then light blue qi and light violet qi (do each color for one minute each). Place your hands over the front aspect of C4 and draw and send light green healing qi into the area as you imagine the healing qi spiraling into the area clockwise, then light violet qi (do each color for one minute each). Place your hands over the back aspect of C3 and draw and send light green healing qi into the area as you imagine the healing qi spiraling into the area clockwise, then light blue qi and light violet qi (do each color for one minute each). Place your hands over the rear aspect of C4 and draw and send light green healing qi into the area as you imagine the healing qi spiraling into the area clockwise, then light violet qi (do each color for one minute each). Draw and send light green qi and light violet qi (alternating colors) into the following areas: C7, C6, the temples (use chicken beak hand position), C5, both sides of the jaw at the joint (use chicken beak hand position), the back of the head (cup skull in hands).

Bladder Infection – Apply local area brushing to C1 (at the base of the tailbone), and the front and back aspect of C2 and C3. Work BL and RN meridians. Place your hands over C1 and draw and send light green healing qi into the area as you imagine the healing qi spiraling into the area clockwise, then light blue qi, and light violet qi (do each color for one minute each). Place your hands first over the front and back aspect of C2 and then the front and back aspect of C3.

Draw and send white healing qi into each chakra while imagining the healing qi spiraling clockwise into the area.

Bleeding – For minor bleeding, cleanse and cover wound. Place hands over the wound (do not touch it) and alternate drawing and sending light green healing qi, light blue healing qi, and white healing qi.

Broken Bones – Do not perform treatment until AFTER bone has been set. Perform localized brushing over area of fracture. Draw and send light blue healing qi into the fracture area. Then alternate drawing and sending light orange and light yellow healing qi into the area.

Burns (Blisters, Sunburn) – For minor burns, blisters or sunburn perform localized brushing over the affected area. Place hands over affected area (do not touch it) and alternate drawing and sending light green healing qi, light blue healing qi, and white healing qi.

Cancer – Perform localized brushing over affected area and C7, C6, back of head, C4, and rear C3. Alternate drawing and sending electric white and electric violet qi into C7, C6, back of head, front aspect of C4, and rear aspect of C3. Draw and send electric white qi and electric violet qi alternatively directly into affected area.

Common Cold (Coughs, Flu, Pleurisy) – Perform localized brushing of sinus and front and back aspect of both lungs. Work LU and RN meridians. Place your hands over the front aspect of C4 and draw and send light green healing qi into the area as you imagine the healing qi spiraling into the area clockwise, then light blue qi and white qi (do each color for one minute each). Place your hands over C1 (the base of the tailbone) and draw and send light green healing qi into the area as you imagine the healing qi spiraling into the area clockwise, then light blue qi and white qi (do each color for one minute each). For head colds, alternate drawing and sending light green healing qi, light blue healing qi, and lastly, white healing qi into C7, C6, and the back of the head. For chest colds or pleurisy, alternate drawing and sending light green healing qi, light blue healing qi, and lastly, white healing qi into C5. Perform direct qi healing technique on the rear aspect of the lungs. One hand should be on the top portion of the left lung and one hand on the top portion of the right lung. Alternative drawing and sending light green, light blue, and then bright white healing qi. Repeat drawing and sending light green, light blue and bright white healing qi into the mid-lung, and then the bottom portion of the lungs.

Constipation – Perform localized brushing of lower abdomen, front and back aspect C3 and C2, and C1 (at the base of the tailbone). Work LI, ST, SP, KI, and RN meridians. Place your hands over C3 and draw and send light green healing qi into the area as you imagine the healing qi spiraling into the area clockwise, then light red qi and white qi (do each color for one minute each). Place your hands over C2 and draw and send light green healing qi into the area as you imagine the healing qi spiraling into the area clockwise, then light orange qi and, light red qi, and white qi (do each color for one minute each). Place your hands over C1 (the base of the tailbone) and draw and send light red healing qi into the area as you imagine the healing qi spiraling into the area clockwise, then white qi (do each color for one minute each).

Cough – See Cold

Cuts – See Bleeding

Cysts - Perform localized brushing over affected area and front and back aspect of C3. Place hands over the cyst and if you can, perform the palm press technique (sandwiching the area between your hands). Alternate drawing and sending light green healing qi, light blue healing qi, and lastly, white healing qi into the area.

Dental and Gum Problems (Mouth Sores, Gingivitis) – Perform localized brushing over the entire mouth and C5. Work ST, LI, SI, SJ, RN, DU meridians. Place hands over C5 and draw and send light green healing qi into the area as you imagine the healing qi spiraling into the area clockwise, then light blue qi and white qi (do each color for one minute each). Using the chicken beak hand position, alternate drawing and sending light green healing qi, light blue healing qi, and lastly, white healing qi along the entire top of the gum line (above the upper lip), and the entire bottom of the gum line.

Diarrhea (Diverticulosis, Loose Stools) – Perform localized brushing over the entire lower abdomen area, front and back aspect of C3 and C2, and C1 (at the base of the tailbone). Work LI, SP, SI, KI, LR, RN meridians. Place your hands over the front aspect of C3 and draw and send light green healing qi, light blue healing qi, and light violet healing qi into the area alternating between each color. Place your hands over the front aspect of C2 and draw and send light green healing qi, light blue healing qi, and light violet healing qi into the area alternating between each color.

Digestive Problems (Indigestion, Gastritis) – Performed localized brushing over the entire front of the abdomen from underneath the breast bone down to the pubic bone, front and back aspect of C4, front and back aspect of C3, and front and back aspect of C2, and C1 (at the base of the tailbone). Work ST, SP, LR, RN, DU meridians. Draw and send light green healing qi, light violet qi, and white qi (alternating between each color) into the following areas: front and back aspect of C4, front and back aspect of C3, front and back aspect of C2, and C1.

Dizziness – Perform localized brushing over the entire front and back of the head. Work HT, GB, DU meridians. Draw and send light green healing qi, light violet qi, and white qi (alternating between each color) into the following areas: C6, C7, and back of the head (cradle skull in hands), and both ears.

Ears (Ear Noise, Tinnitus) – Perform localized brushing over the entire front and back of the head and C5. Work LI, SI, BL, SJ, GB, DU meridians. Using the Laser Finger hand position (with tip of index finger just inside the opening of the affected ear(s)) draw and send light blue healing qi, light green qi, light orange qi, light red qi, and white qi (alternating between each color) into the affected ear(s).

Energizer Treatment – Work RN, DU meridians. Place one hand on C3 and one hand on the dantian (at C2). Draw and send white healing qi into the area. Draw and send white healing qi into C6, and C7, and the back of the head (cradle skull in your hands).

Eyes – For basic eye or vision problems perform localized brushing of eyes, C6, C7, and the back of the head. Work ST, SI, BL, SJ, GB meridians. Place both of your hands over the eyes and draw and send light green healing qi into the area as you imagine the healing qi spiraling into the area clockwise, then light yellow qi, light violet qi and light blue qi (do each color for one minute each). Place your hands over C6 and draw and send light green healing qi into the area as you imagine the healing qi spiraling into the area clockwise, then light yellow qi, light violet qi and light blue qi (do each color for one minute each). Place your hands over C7 and draw and send light green healing qi into the area as you imagine the healing qi spiraling into the area clockwise, then light yellow qi, light violet qi and light blue qi (do each color for one minute each). Place your hands over the back of the head (cup the skull in your hands) and draw and send light violet healing qi into the area, then white healing qi. Place your hands over the eyes and draw and send light green healing qi, light yellow qi, light violet qi and light blue qi, alternating between each color.

Feet and Toes – For general muscular or joint pain in the feet and toes, apply local brushing over area of discomfort, brushing downwards (past the toes). For pain in the sole of the foot work the KI meridian. For the big toe work the SP meridian. For the second toe work the ST meridian. For the fourth toe work the GB meridian. For the little toe work the BL meridian. Place your dominant hand over C1 (area over coccyx) and draw and send white healing qi into the area as you move the palm of your hand in a clockwise motion (do this for one minute). If you sensed heat in the area affected or if there is inflammation, place the palm of your hand over the area and move the palm of your dominant hand in a counter clockwise motion (ten passes) with the intention of taking out excess qi energy. Perform paint brush hand technique over the area as you draw and send light green qi and then light blue qi. Sandwich affected body part between the palms and perform Direct Qi Healing continuing to draw and send light green and light blue qi into the area.

Fever – Make sure that you have done a thorough job brushing the front and back of the entire body. Work LU, DU meridians. Draw and send light green healing qi, light blue qi, and light violet qi (alternating between each color) into the following areas: C5, C6, C7, front and back aspect of C4, front and back aspect of C3, front and back aspect of C2, and back of the head (cradle skull in hands).

Flu – See Cold

Food Poisoning – Perform localized brushing over entire abdominal area, C3, and C2. Work LI, ST, SP, SI, LR, GB meridians. Draw and send light green healing qi, light blue qi, and white qi (alternating between each color) into the following areas: C3 and C2.

Hand and Fingers – For general muscular or joint pain in the hand or fingers, apply local brushing over area of discomfort, brushing downwards (towards the fingers). For hand pain work HT, SI, PC meridians. For little finger work the HT meridian. For the ring finger work the SJ meridian. For the middle finger work the PC meridian. For the thumb work the LU meridian. For the index finger work the LI meridian. Place your dominant hand over C4 and draw and send white healing qi into the area as you move the palm of your hand in a clockwise motion (do this for one minute). If you sensed heat in the area affected or if there is inflammation, place the palm of your hand over the area and move the palm of your dominant hand in a counter clockwise motion (ten passes) with the intention of taking out excess qi energy. Perform paint brush hand technique over the area as you draw and send light green qi and then light blue qi. Sandwich affected body part between the palms and perform Direct Qi Healing continuing to draw and send light green and light blue qi into the area.

Headache Migraine - Perform localized brushing over front and back of head, front and back aspect of C3, front and back aspect of C4, liver area, entire length of spinal column, and C1 (at the base of the tailbone). Work LI, SI, BL, SJ, GB, DU meridians. Place your hands over the front aspect of C3 and draw and send light green healing qi into the area as you imagine the healing qi spiraling into the area clockwise, then light blue qi and light violet qi (do each color for one minute each). Place your hands over the front aspect of C4 and draw and send light green healing qi into the area as you imagine the healing qi spiraling into the area clockwise, then light violet qi (do each color for one minute each). Place your hands over the back aspect of C3 and draw and send light green healing qi into the area as you imagine the healing qi spiraling into the area clockwise, then light blue qi and light violet qi (do each color for one minute each). Place your hands over the rear aspect of C4 and draw and send light green healing qi into the area as you imagine the healing qi spiraling into the area clockwise, then light violet qi (do each color for one minute each). Draw and send light green healing qi, light blue qi, and light violet qi (alternating between each color) into the following areas: C5, C6, C7, and back of the head (cradle skull in hands).

Headache Tension – Perform localized brushing over front and back of head, and entire length of spinal column. Work LI, SI, BL, SJ, GB, DU meridians. Draw and send light green healing qi, light blue qi, and light violet qi (alternating between each color) into the following areas: C5, C6, C7, and back of the head (cradle skull in hands).

Heart Burn – See Digestive Problems

High Blood Pressure – Perform localized brushing of entire front and back of head, entire length of the spinal column, front and back aspect of C3, and front and back aspect of C4. Work BL meridian. Draw and send light green healing qi, light blue qi, and light violet qi (alternating between each color) into the following areas: front and back aspect C4, the sides of the throat, and the back of the head (cradle skull in hands).

Kidney Infection – Perform localized brushing of kidneys (through the back), front and back aspect of C2, front and back aspect of C3, and C1 (at the base of the skull). Work ST. BL, KI meridians. Place your hands on the kidneys (through the back) and draw and send light green healing qi, light orange qi, and white qi into the area. Wait a few minutes, then draw and send light green healing qi, light blue qi, and light violet qi (alternating between colors) into the kidneys. Draw and send white healing qi into the following areas: front and back aspect of C3, front and back aspect of C4, and C1.

Laryngitis (Sore Throat) – Perform localized brushing of entire front and back of head and neck, and front and back aspect of C4. Work LI, SI, ST, SJ meridians. Draw and send light green healing qi, light blue qi, and light violet qi (alternating between each color) into the following areas: front and back aspect of C5.

Leg Pain – For general muscular or joint pain in the leg, apply local brushing over the area of discomfort, brushing downwards (towards the foot). For ankle pain work the BL and KI meridians. For pain in the calves work the BL, and SP meridian. For shin pain work the ST meridian. For thighs/quadriceps work SI, SP. LR, GB meridians. For hamstring pain work the LI meridian. For knee pain work ST, SP, BL, KI, LR, GB meridians. Place your dominant hand over C1 (area over coccyx) and draw and send white healing qi into the area as you move the palm of your hand in a clockwise motion (do this for one minute). If you sensed heat in the area affected or if there is inflammation, place the palm of your hand over the area and move the palm of your dominant hand in a counter clockwise motion (ten passes) with the intention of taking out excess qi energy. Perform paint brush hand technique over the area as you draw and send light green qi and then light blue qi. Sandwich affected body part between the palms and perform Direct Qi Healing continuing to draw and send light green and light blue qi into the area.

Liver Infections – Perform localized brushing of entire liver area, front and back aspect of C3, and spleen. Work LR meridian. Place your hands on front C3, draw and send light green healing qi, light blue qi, and light violet qi (alternating between colors). Draw and send white healing qi into the spleen.

Lung Infections (Pneumonia, Bronchitis) - Apply local area brushing over the front and back aspect of both lungs, and on liver area. Work the LU, and RN meridians. Place your hands over the front aspect of C4 and draw and send light green healing qi into the area as you imagine the healing qi spiraling into the area clockwise, then light blue qi and white qi (do each color for one minute each). Place your hands over the front aspect of C3 and draw and send light green healing qi into the area as you imagine the healing qi spiraling into the area clockwise, then light blue qi and white qi (do each color for one minute each). Place your hands over the rear aspect of C4 and draw and send light green healing qi into the area as you imagine the healing qi spiraling into the area clockwise, then light blue qi and white qi (do each color for one minute each). Place your hands over the rear aspect of C3 and draw and send light green healing qi into the area as you imagine the healing qi spiraling into the area clockwise, then light blue qi and white qi (do each color for one minute each). Perform direct qi healing technique on the rear aspect of the lungs. One hand should be on the top portion of the left lung and one hand on the top portion of the right lung. Alternative drawing and sending light green, light blue, and then bright white healing qi. Repeat drawing and sending light green, light blue and bright white healing qi into the mid-lung, and then the bottom portion of the lungs.

Menstrual Problems (PMS, Cramps) – Perform localized brushing of lower abdomen, low back, and front and rear aspect of C2. Work ST and SP meridians. Place your hands over the front aspect of C2 and draw and send light green healing qi into the area as you imagine the healing qi spiraling into the area clockwise, then light orange qi and white qi (do each color for one minute each). Place your hands over the back aspect of C2 and draw and send light green healing qi into the area as you imagine the healing qi spiraling into the area clockwise, then light orange qi and white qi (do each color for one minute each).

Nausea – Perform localized brushing of entire abdominal area from bottom of breastbone to pubic area, and back aspect of C3. Work ST, LI, SI, RN meridians. Draw and send light green healing qi, light blue qi, and light violet qi (alternating between each color) into the following areas: front C3, and C2.

Neck Pain – For general neck pain, apply local brushing over area of discomfort, brushing downwards (towards the fingers). Work ST, SI, SJ, GB, DU meridians. Place your dominant hand over C5 and draw and send white healing qi into the area as you move the palm of your hand in a clockwise motion (do this for one minute). If you sensed heat in the area affected or if there is inflammation, place the palm of your hand over the area and move the palm of your dominant hand in a counter clockwise motion (ten passes) with the intention of taking out excess qi energy. Perform paint brush hand technique over the area as you draw and send light green qi and then light blue qi. Sandwich affected body part between the palms and perform Direct Qi Healing continuing to draw and send light green and light blue qi into the area.

Relaxing Treatment – Perform localized brushing on the front and back of the head and neck, C3, and C1 (at the base of the tailbone). Work HT, GB meridians. Draw and send light blue healing qi into C3. Draw and send white healing qi into C2.

Sciatica – See Back Ache

Shoulder Pain – For general muscular or joint pain in the shoulder, upper back, and trapezius, apply local brushing over area of discomfort, brushing downwards (towards the fingers). Work the LU, SI, BL, SJ, and GB meridians. Place your dominant hand over C4 and draw and send white healing qi into the area as you move the palm of your hand in a clockwise motion (do this for one minute). If you sensed heat in the area affected or if there is inflammation, place the palm of your hand over the area and move the palm of your dominant hand in a counter clockwise motion (ten passes) with the intention of taking out excess qi energy. Perform paint brush hand technique over the area as you draw and send light green qi and then light blue qi. Sandwich affected body part between the palms and perform Direct Qi Healing continuing to draw and send light green and light blue qi into the area.

Sinus Problems – Perform localized brushing of front and back of head and neck, front and back aspect of C3, and back aspect of C4. Work LU meridian. Place your hands over the front aspect of C3 and draw and send light green healing qi into the area as you imagine the healing qi spiraling into the area clockwise, then light blue qi and light violet qi (do each color for one minute each). Place your hands over the front aspect of C4 and draw and send light green healing qi into the area as you imagine the healing qi spiraling into the area clockwise, then light violet qi (do each color for one minute each). Place your hands over the rear aspect of C4 and draw and send light green healing qi into the area as you imagine the healing qi spiraling into the area clockwise, then light violet qi (do each color for one minute each). Draw and send light green healing qi, light blue qi, and light violet qi (alternating between each color) into the following areas: front and back C5, C6, C7, and back of the head (cradle skull in hands).

Skin Problems (Rash, Acne) – Perform localized brushing over the affected area, C1 (at the base of the tailbone), front and back aspect of C2, front and back aspect of C3, C5, C6, and the back of the head (cradle skull in hands). Work ST meridian. Draw and send light green healing qi, and light violet qi (alternating between each color) into the following areas: front and back C3, C5, C6, and back of the head (cradle skull in hands). Draw and send white healing qi into front and back aspect of C2, and C1. Using paint brush hand technique draw and send light green healing qi, light blue qi, light violet qi, and pink qi over the affected area.

Sprain/Strain - See affected body part.

TMJ (Temporal-Mandibular Joint Dysfunction) – Performed localized brushing of front and back of head and neck (including both sides of the face at the jaw area). Work SI meridian. Perform paintbrush hand technique directly over Temporal-Mandibular Joints (right in front of ears) as you draw ands send light green healing qi and light blue healing qi. Perform direct healing using chicken beak hand technique drawing and sending light green healing qi, and light blue qi (alternating between each color) into both jaw joints.

Tonsillitis – See Laryngitis

Tumors, Benign – Perform localized brushing of affected area, C6, front and back aspect of C4, front and back aspect of C3, and C1 (at the base of the tailbone). Alternate drawing and sending electric white and electric violet qi into C6, and directly into affected area performing the palm press technique (sandwiching the area between your hands) if you can, alternating between each color.

Vomiting – See Diarrhea

Wellness Treatment – The instructions for a general wellness treatment can be found in the chapter The Jing-QI-Shen Treatment Session. For a general wellness treatment perform steps one through four, skipping step five, and proceeding to step six.

Appendix B:

MERIDIAN - DISEASE RELATIONSHIPS

Meridian	Associated symptoms
Lung (LU)	Respiratory diseases, bronchitis, pleurisy, pneumonia, swollen and/or sore throat, cough, shortness of breath, pain in chest, fever, common cold, flu, chest fullness, acid based (alkaline) imbalances, wrist pain, thumb stiffness or pain, pain in the shoulder and along meridian path.
Large Intestine/ Colon (LI)	Swollen face, hearing difficulty, headache, abdominal pain, constipation, diarrhea, vomiting, swollen and/or sore throat, toothache in the lower gum, herpes simplex on lips, nasal discharge, nasal bleeding, pain in hamstring, pain in the forearm, wrist, elbow, or along meridian path.
Stomach (ST)	Stomach problems, gastritis, indigestion, abdominal pain, abdominal distension, constipation, colitis, edema, vomiting, sore throat, facial paralysis, upper gum toothache, teeth grinding, esophagus disorders, diaphragm disorders, acne, blurred vision, redness and swelling of eye, asthma, chronic fatigue syndrome, fibromyalgia, ovary dysfunctions, appendicitis, diabetes, gallstones, pancreatitis, hypo/hyperglycemia, acid based (alkaline) imbalances, peptic ulcer, Crohn's disease, cirrhosis, kidney or adrenal glad dysfunctions, neck pain, knee pain, shin splints, shin pain, aches and pain along meridian path.
Spleen (SP)	Problems of the spleen and pancreas, indigestion, diarrhea, vomiting, bowel problems, abdominal distension, constipation, uterine bleeding, uterine fibroids, endometriosis, fallopian tube dysfunctions, menstrual abnormalities, thyroid problems, prostate problems, heart palpitations, diabetes mellitus, thigh pain, medial aspect knee pain, pain in the latissimus dorsi muscles, pain in the triceps muscle, trapezius muscle pain, pain and/or stiffness of the big toe, pain along meridian path.
Heart (HT)	Heart problems, angina pectoris, chest pains, heart palpitations, numbness, pain or stiffness of the hand and arm, pain in armpits, wrist pain, pain or stiffness in the little finger, dryness of the throat, stiffness in tongue, stuttering, retinal hemorrhages, insomnia, sleep apnea, pain along meridian path.
Small Intestine (SI)	Lower abdominal pain, diarrhea, colitis, blurred vision, swollen and sore throat, swelling or paralysis of face, swollen lymph nodes in cervical neck region, heart disorders, tinnitus, deafness, ear disorders, hand and wrist pain, stiff neck, headache, shoulder, arm, elbow pain, TMJ, tooth-

	ache, quadriceps weakness or pain, pain along the meridian path.
Bladder (BL)	Bladder and kidney problems, urinary frequency, painful urination, chronic cystitis, headache, swollen eyes, blurred vision, vision disorders, loss of hearing, ear disorders, headaches, stiff or painful neck, cervical curving, abdominal pain, shoulder and back pain, chest pain, hypo/hypertension, jaundice, irregular menses, sciatica, scoliosis, general low back pain, lumbar spine strain, pain behind knee and back of the leg, cramping in calves, ankle sprain, ankle edema, Achilles tendonitis, pain along meridian path.
Kidney(KI)	Kidney problems, low back pain, slipped spinal discs L1-5, sacrum and coccyx pain, osteomyelitis, osteoporosis, fullness and pain in lower abdomen, abdominal distention, shortness of breath, panic attacks, heart failure, parathyroid dysfunctions, cough, fullness in chest, phlegm, external genital pain, prostate and uterine dysfunctions, nocturnal emissions, sexual dysfunction, pink urine, painful urination, constipation, vomiting, diarrhea, dorsal knee pain, ankle sprain, ankle edema, medial calf pain, burning sensation or pain on the sole of the foot, pain along meridian path.
Pericardium(PC)	Cardiac pain, suffocating sensation in the chest, poor circulation, angina pectoris, palpitation, nausea, vomiting, dizziness, elbow and arm pain, painful, swollen arm pits, hot, sweaty palms, wrist pain, pain or stiffness in the middle finger, tremor of hand and arm, chest pain, stomach ache, pain in the gluteus maximus, or adductor muscles, pain along meridian path.
Sanjiao Meridian (SJ) (Triple Warmer)	Deafness, tinnitus, ear problems, sore throat, abdominal distension, facial nerve disorders, swelling of cheek and facial muscles, blurred vision, migraine, heart disorders, hypothalamus, pineal and pituitary disorders, hot flashes, cold chills, urinary incontinence, neck and shoulder pain, elbow pain, wrist pain, pain or stiffness in the ring finger, headache, toothache, irritability, pain along meridian path.
Liver (LR)	Liver problems, jaundice, hepatitis, Alzheimer's disease, memory loss, depression, lower abdominal pain, painful urination, external genital pain, lumbago, vomiting, diarrhea, indigestion, acid regurgitation, esophagus disorders, heart burn, thyroid disorders, bad breath, pituitary and hypothalamus dysfunctions, hernia, sexual disorders and dysfunctions, urination problems, lower abdominal pain, pain in medial aspect of knee and thigh, pain in the lower abdomen, lower abdominal distention, pain along meridian path.

Gall Bladder (GB)	Gall bladder problems, tinnitus, blurred vision, vertigo, pain and stiffness in the neck, shoulder and upper back pain, headache, migraine, pain in lumbar region and thigh, swelling and pain in the knee, jaundice, vomiting, irregular menstruation, abdominal pain, weakness and numbness in the lower extremities, sleeping disorders, pain along meridian path.
Ren Mai (RN) (Conceptual)	Lower abdominal pain, urinary frequency, urinary retention, irregular menstruation, morbid leukorrhea, uterine bleeding, indigestion, diarrhea, constipation, nausea, vomiting, hiccup, prolapse of rectum, hernia, distention and fullness in chest and costal region, chest pain, cough, breathing difficulties, swollen gums, toothache, and facial puffiness.
Du Mai (DU) (Governing)	Pain and stiffness in the neck, back pain, lumbago, low back pain and stiffness, irregular menstruation, prolapse of rectum, prolapse of vagina, indigestion, leukorrhea, spinal problems, mental disorders, fever, headaches, vertigo, tinnitus, lip twitching, pain and swelling of gums.

Appendix C:

Meridian Illustrations With Xue Points

Abbreviations of the Fourteen Meridians:

Lung Meridian (LU)
Large Intestine Meridian (LI)
Stomach Meridian (ST)
Spleen Meridian (SP)
Heart Meridian (HT)
Small Intestine Meridian (SI)
Urinary Bladder Meridian (BL)
Kidney Meridian (KI)
Pericardium Meridian (PC)
Sanjiao Meridian (SJ)
Liver Meridian (LI)
Gall Bladder Meridian (GB)
Ren Mai Meridian (RN)
Du Mai Meridian (DU)

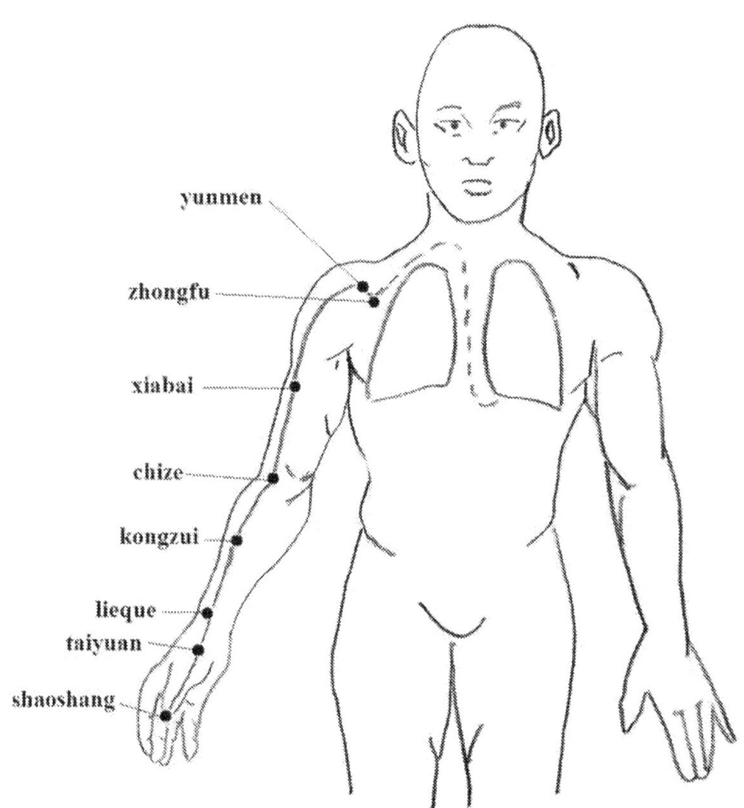

Lung Meridian

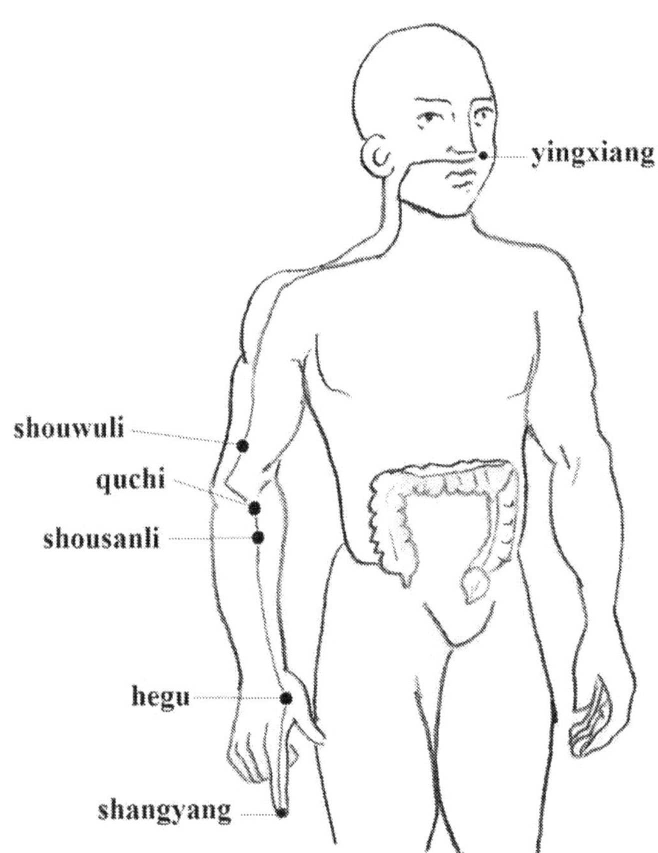

Large Intestine/Colon Meridian

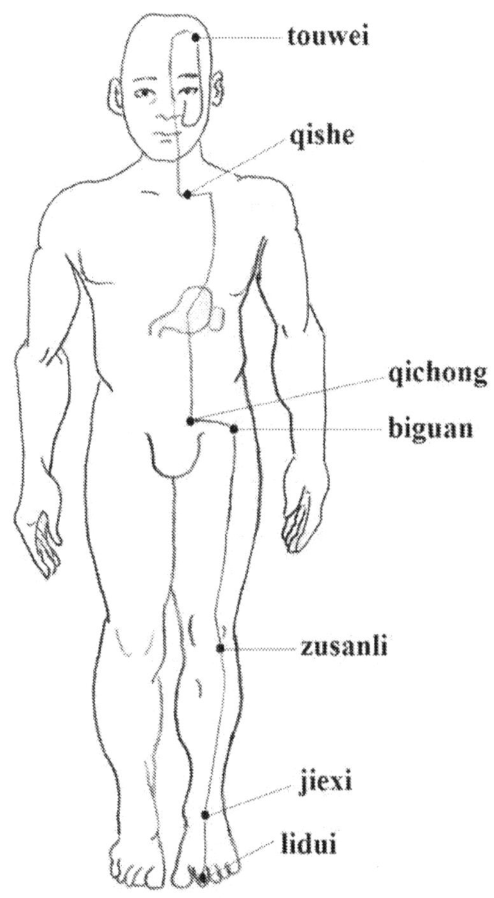

Stomach Meridian

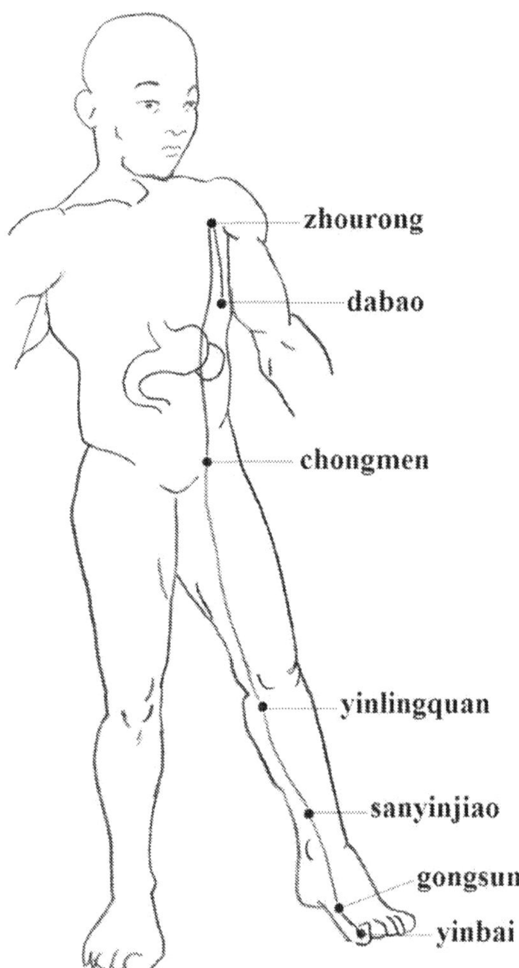

Spleen Meridian

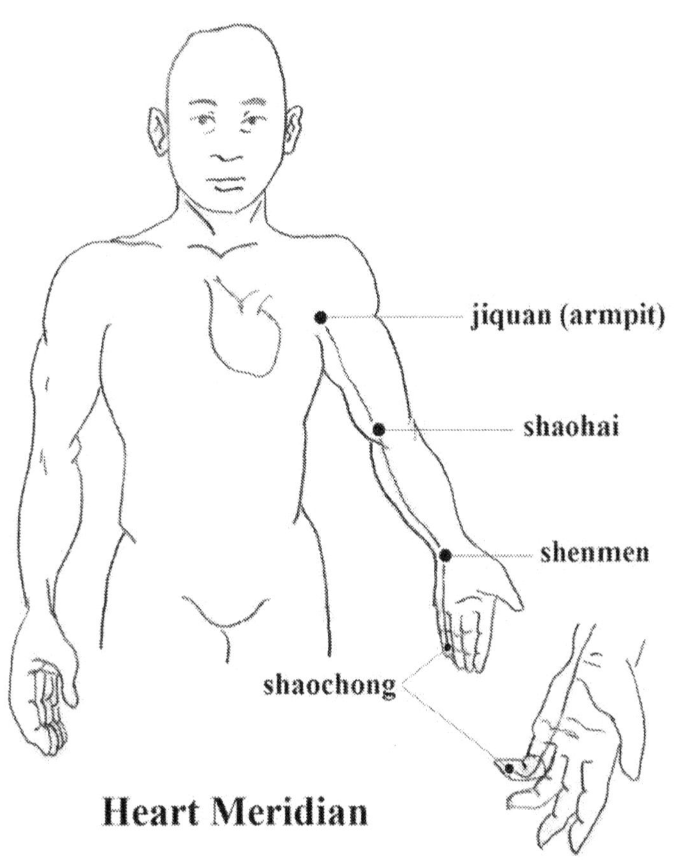

Heart Meridian

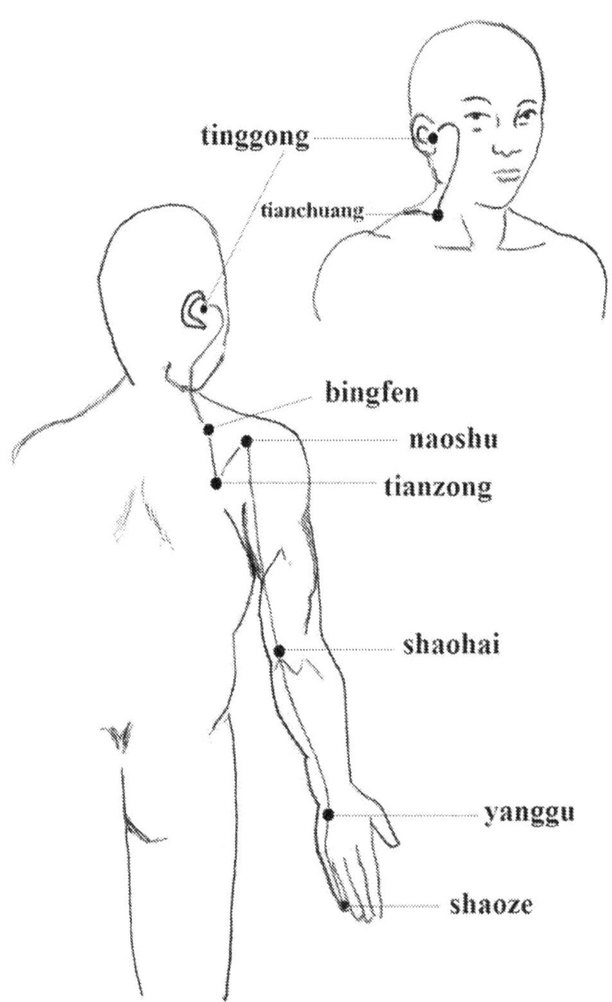

Small Intestine Meridian

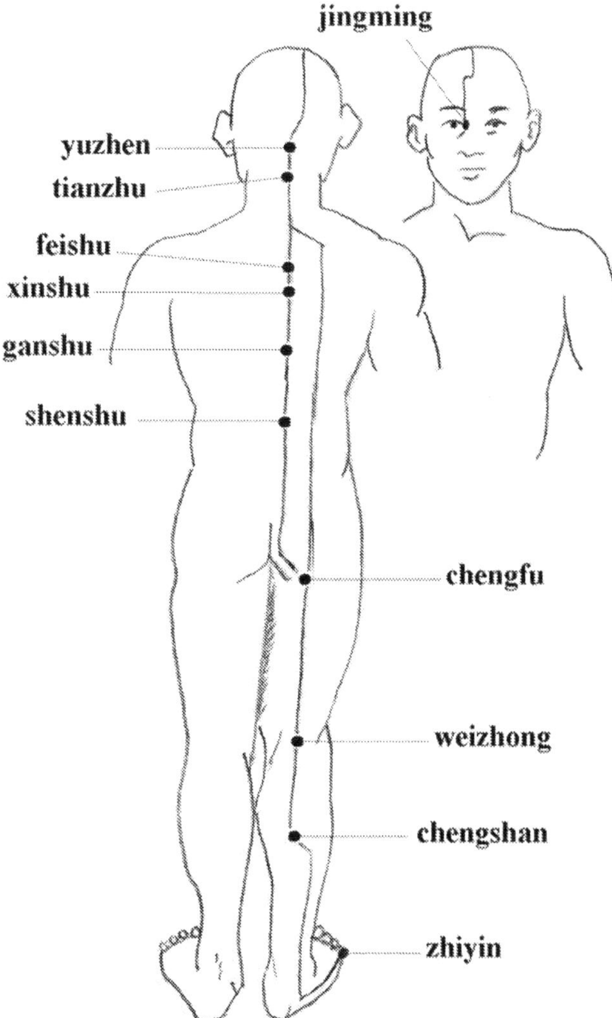

Urinary Bladder Meridian

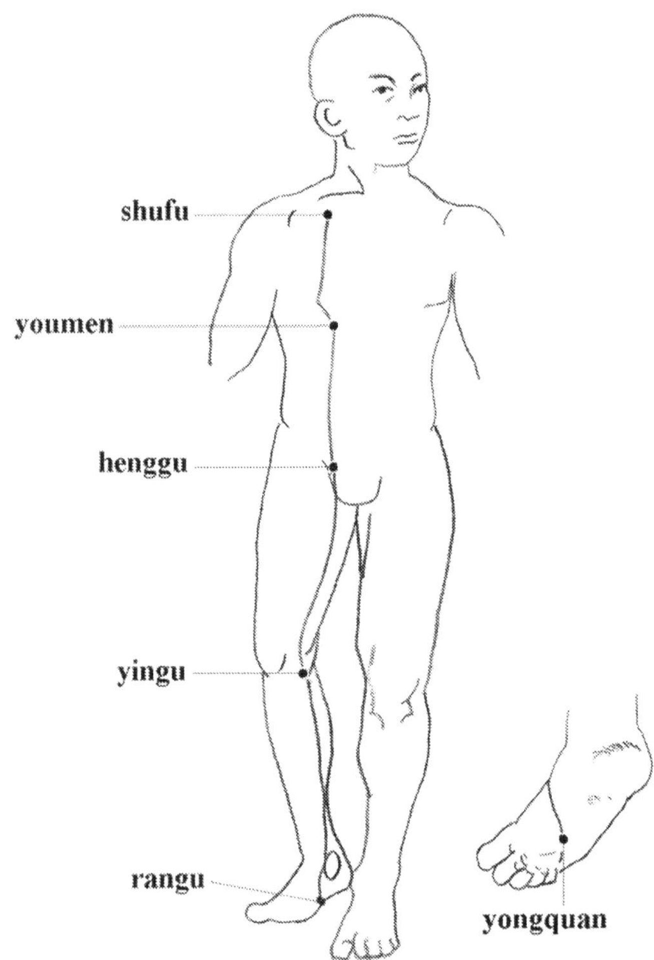

Kidney Meridian

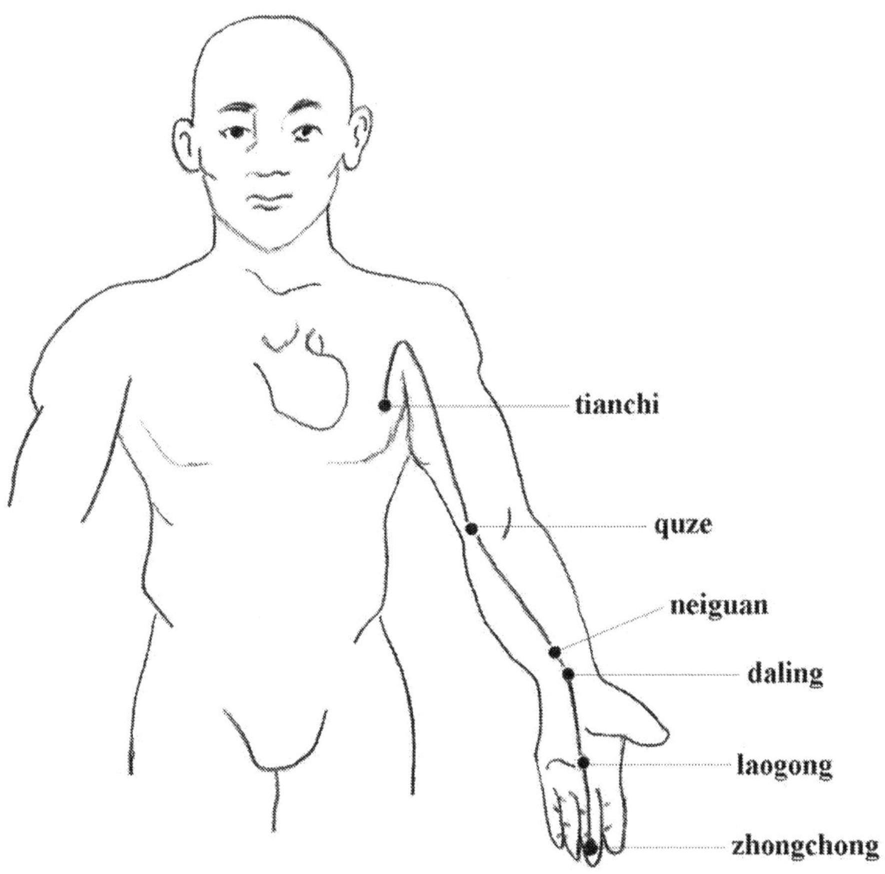

Pericardium Meridian

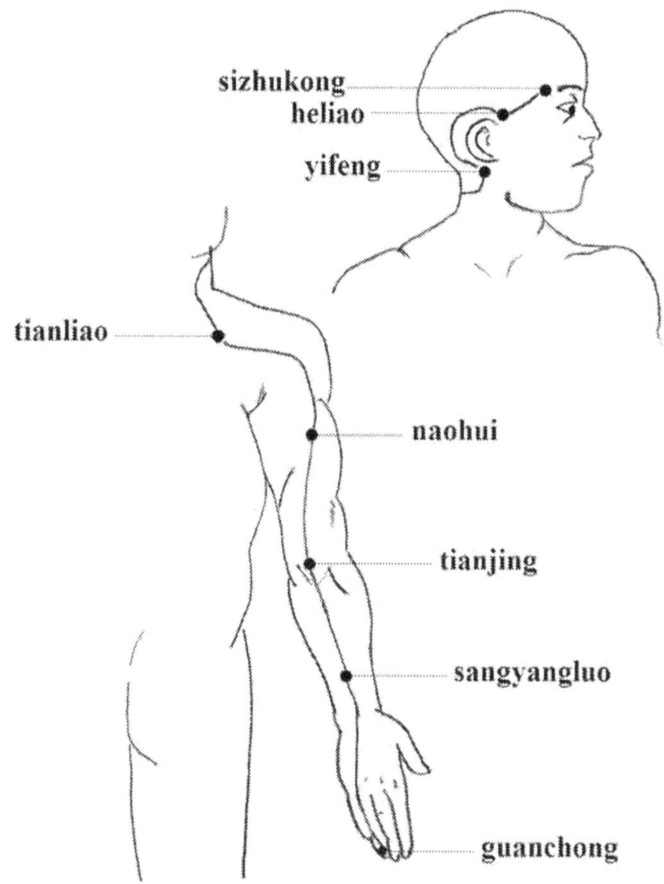

Sanjiao (Triple Warmer) Meridian

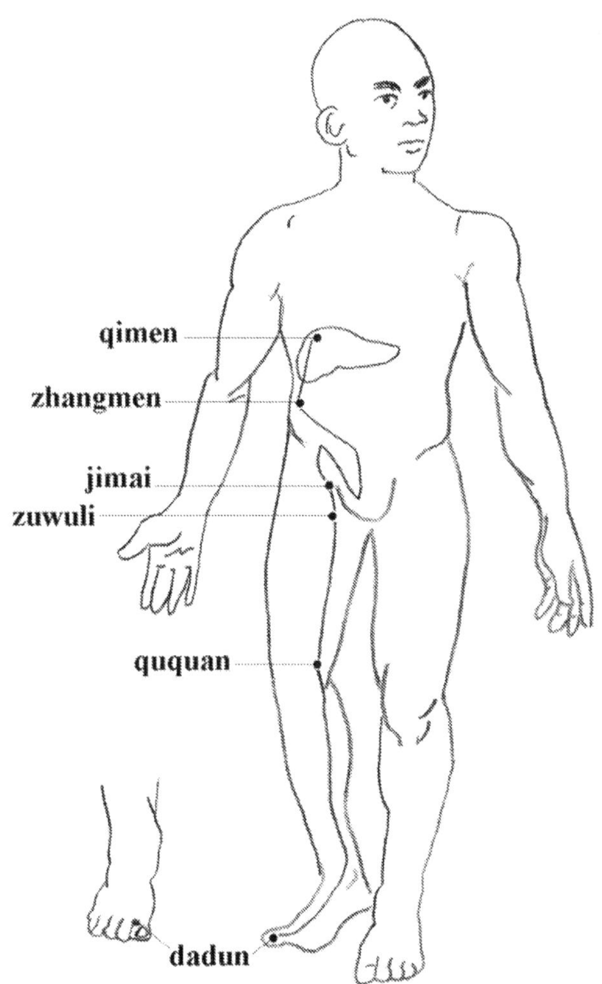

Liver Meridian

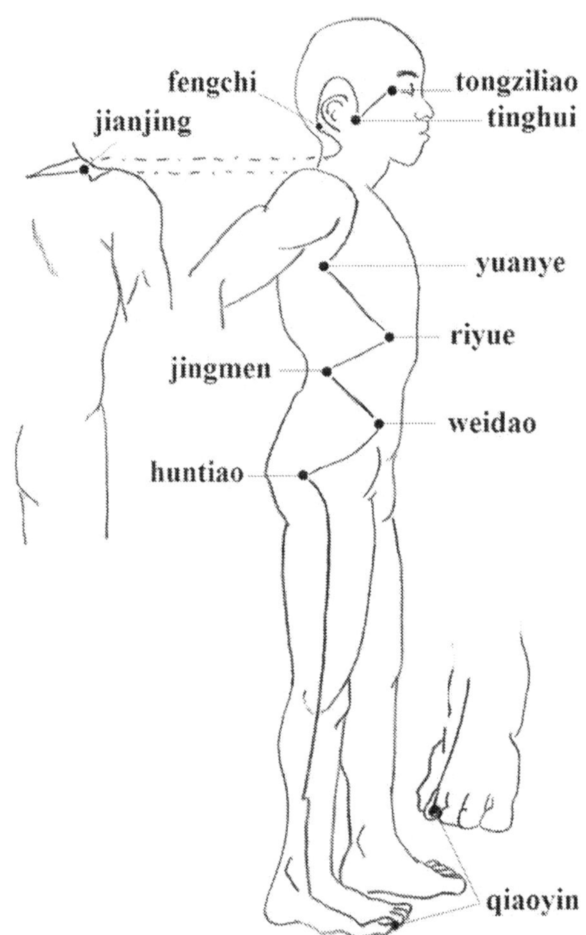

Gall Bladder Meridian

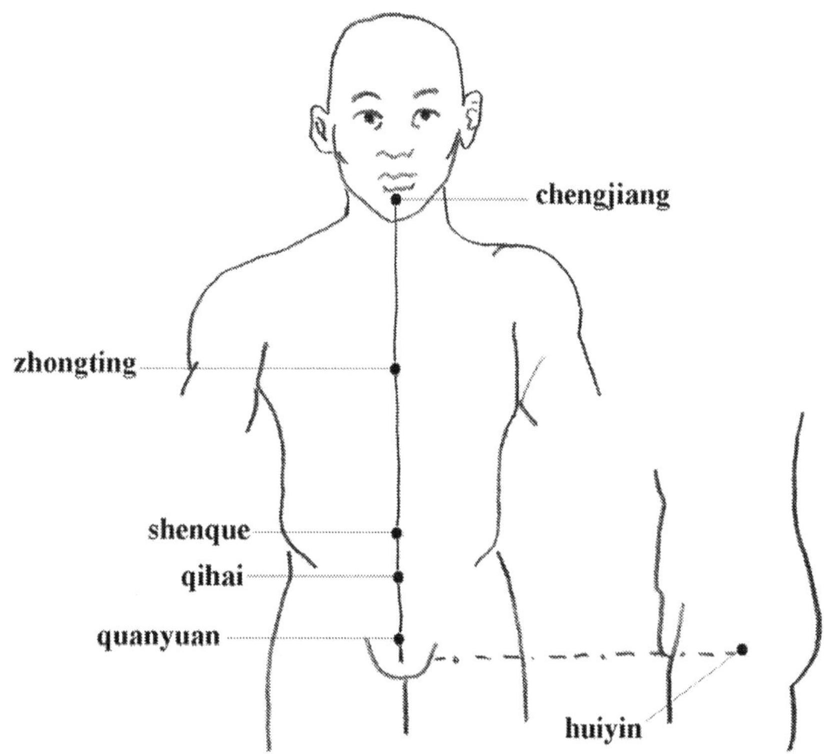

Ren Mai Meridian

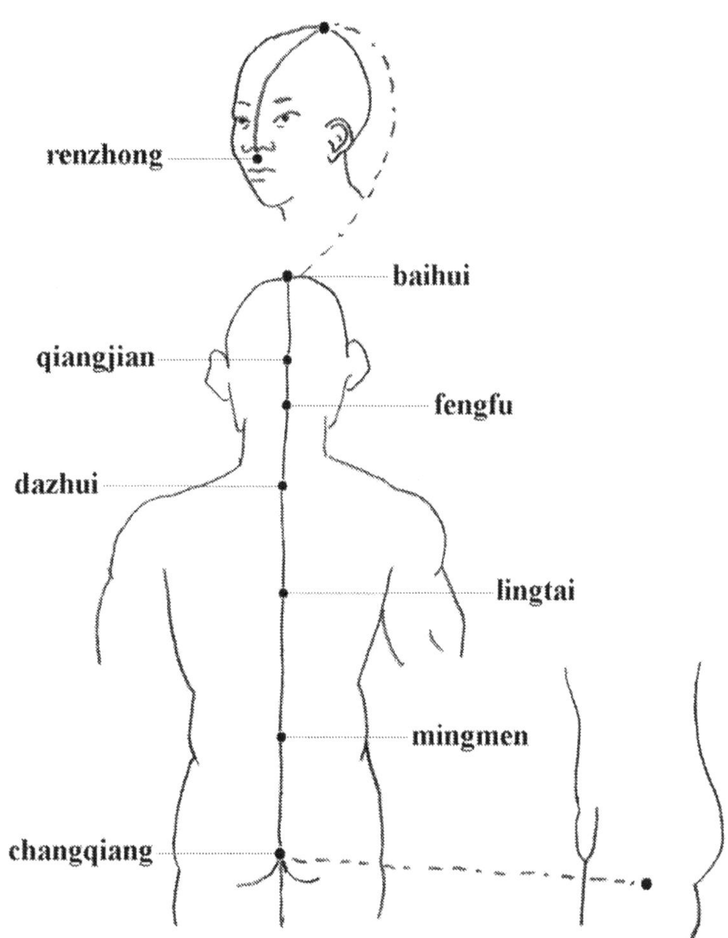

Du Mai Meridian

Lightning Source UK Ltd.
Milton Keynes UK
UKOW07f1354030517
300395UK00002B/14/P

9 780615 136950